STUDIES IN AFRICAN AMERICAN HISTORY AND CULTURE

edited by

GRAHAM HODGES
COLGATE UNIVERSITY

A GARLAND SERIES

IDENTITY, FAMILY, AND FOLKLORE IN AFRICAN AMERICAN LITERATURE

LEE ALFRED WRIGHT

GARLAND PUBLISHING, Inc.
New York & London / 1995

Library of Congress Cataloging-in-Publication Data

Wright, Lee Alfred, 1951–
    Identity, family, and folklore in African American literature / Lee
Alfred Wright.
      p.   cm. — (Studies in African American history and culture)
    Includes bibliographical references and index.
    ISBN 0–8153–1864–2
    1. American literature—Afro-American authors—History and criti-
cism.   2. Identity (Psychology) in literature.   3. Afro-Americans in
literature.   4. Folklore in literature.   5. Family in literature.
I. Title.   II. Series.
PS153.N5W75   1995
810.9'353—dc20   94–33569
                                                                              CIP

Printed on acid-free, 250-year-life paper
Manufactured in the United States of America

For my wife, Beth Ann Nancarrow-Wright, and my daughters Amy, Brittany, and Caitlin.

CONTENTS

ACKNOWLEDGEMENTS

I want to thank Professors Thomas Barden, Guy Szuberla and James Saunders for reading and making suggestions about this work, especially in its early stages.

INTRODUCTION

This work examines the integrity of personal and family identity as it has been defined and challenged in African American literature, primarily in fiction, from the mid-nineteenth century to the present.

An early focus of this study is the literary documentation of the break up of black families beginning with depictions of slavery, and the slaves' response to this callous disregard of their family bonds. Of major importance also is the depiction of the family in African American literature of the twentieth century.

After the Civil War, the African American family did not quickly coalesce; its break up continued and has, in fact, persisted to this day. Not surprisingly, the disintegration of the black family has been a central theme in African American literature. This work will examine the theme in detail. It is not, however, comprehensive, nor was it intended to be. I have selected representative works, each well-known and emblematic. Furthermore, because African American writers have made use of their own culture's folklore as one way of defining both personal and family identity within the black community, the thematic use of folklore will also be a major concern of this study.

Beginning with William Wells Brown's *Clotel*[1] (1853), a work which is generally considered the first novel written by an African American,[2] this study moves to Charles Chesnutt's *The Conjure Woman*[3] (1899), focusing upon the literary record of the break up of black families under slavery and the ways blacks responded to the callous disregard of their family bonds during those times. This work then takes an intensive look at four novels by two modern women writers, Alice Walker and Toni Morrison. Walker's *Meridian* and *The Color Purple*, and Morrison's *The Bluest Eye* and *Sula* are analyzed for their use of folklore and/or the blues as a way of defining character, personal identity and cultural rootedness.[4] A number of other works are drawn upon also, including Harriet Jacobs' *Incidents in the Life of a Slave Girl* (1861) and Ann Petry's *The Street* (1946), both of which helped to establish a literary record of the self-sacrificing African American mother.[5]

Of major interest to this study are the ways folklore has been used to define personal identity in African American literature and the way the blues has been employed to signify meaning in African American fiction. The blues are a prominent component of African American folklore, and because the idiom of the blues informs a number of African American fictional works, blues considerations are very much central to the works to be considered.

That the first two novels in this study were written by men and the latter four by women is more an act of chance than deliberate formulation on my part. Matters of point of view and sexual roles as they relate to individual and family identity do result in obvious differences in these works, and are addressed when significant, but these were not matters of central importance to me when choosing them.

Another notable difference between the earlier and latter works is that of each writer's intended audience. Most African American writers from the eighteenth century until the time period separating WWI and WWII (from Phillis Wheatley to at least Richard Wright and James Baldwin) were writing primarily for white audiences, a fact which influenced the form, content, and intent of their writings.[6] The writers of slave narratives and other antebellum literature were subject especially to the propagandist exigencies of the abolitionist presses.[7] Even after the Civil War, the goal of assimilation into the larger white American society helped mold the content and intent of many black writers' works. The so-called protest novel of the middle twentieth century is no different. Although novels by African American writers still retain the power to stir political debate today and provide a forum for the discussion of race relations, the necessity of "masking" is no longer an overbearing concern for modern African American writers.

That early African American writers felt compelled to "mask" their true feelings from their white audiences, or to completely evade particularly sensitive issues, leads naturally to questions of the complete reliability and honesty of those earlier texts. Critics need to be aware of this issue not only in the study of primary sources, but in the study of secondary sources as well. Zora Neale Hurston, for instance, suggests in *Mules and Men* (1935), that the authenticity and reliability of folklore sources could be greatly compromised by the expectations of the collector:

Folk-lore is not as easy to collect as it sounds. The best source is where there are the least outside influences and these people, being usually under-privileged, are the shyest. They are most reluctant at times to reveal that which the soul lives by. And the Negro, in spite of his open-faced laughter, his seeming acquiescence, is particularly evasive. You see we are a polite people and we do not say to our questioner: "Get out of here!" We smile and tell him or her something that satisfies the white person because, knowing so little about us, he doesn't know what he is missing.[8]

From Hurston's comment, it can be inferred that the assumption of a "mask" when in the presence of outsiders, is a folk posture common to the "under-privileged." "Double-consciousness," as W.E.B. DuBois labelled it in *The Souls of Black Folk* (1903) was not, however, restricted to the lower classes of African Americans; even the Talented Tenth, as DuBois labelled the educated elite, were subject to double-consciousness.[9] Ralph Ellison claimed that, even as late as 1964, the time he penned his introduction to *Shadow and Act*, the persistence of the literary mask was still a problem for the black writer:

...I found the greatest difficulty for a Negro writer was the problem of revealing what he truly felt, rather than serving up what Negroes were supposed to feel, and were encouraged to feel. And linked to this was the difficulty, based upon our long habit of deception and evasion, of depicting what really happened within our areas of American life, and putting down with honesty and without bowing to ideological expediencies the attitudes and values which give Negro American life its sense of wholeness and which render it bearable and human and, when measured by our own terms, desirable.[10]

No doubt the need to mask in part explains the development of a discourse within the African American community which by necessity was double-voiced and relied upon the act of signifying.

According to Houston Baker, only with the rise of black consciousness and a sense of a black aesthetic beginning in the 1960s has it been possible for black writers to write to and for their own people, without primary consideration of a white audience or Western ideals. Baker writes in *The Journey Back*:

> In sum, black writers of the fifties were not certain they had a country. They worked, perhaps too often, in a world of abstractions that included not only their most esteemed values, but also their hypothetical, or implied, Western audience. In the sixties and seventies, on the other hand, black spokesmen were convinced that their real audience, like the nation to come, was black, and their values and canons were designed to accord with this conviction.[11]

There are exceptions, certainly. Nonetheless, there does appear to be agreement that, for the most part, African American writers needed to be keenly aware of the cultural and racial sensitivities of their white audiences when they wrote, at least until the mid-twentieth century.

In addition to considerations of the author's gender and audience, another difference that exists between the two sets of novels under consideration in this work is the proliferation of the blues, and its use as a trope in African American works. The spread of the blues out of the "delta" where they originated occurred sometime during the 1910s and 1920s as southern blacks began the movement out of the rural south and into the industrialized, urban north. LeRoi Jones' socio-historical study, *Blues People*, documents that migration: "At the turn of the century most Negroes still lived in rural areas of the South, but by 1914 the largest exodus began. Masses of Negroes began to move to the Northern industrial centers such as Chicago, Detroit, New York."[12] This migration north resulted in the concurrent spread of the blues and is significant not only because the blues are a part of African American folklore, but because the idiom of the blues, the philosophy of and expression of life's experiences which makes the blues distinctive, inform a number of African American fictional works.[13] As shall be shown, even in the nineteenth century works under consideration, the blues are ever-present, although that presence is subtextual. Only in the twentieth century are the blues employed consciously to characterize protagonists and thereby signify upon their cultural grounding.

All of the above factors--a writer's sex, his/her intended audience, the political climate the work appears in, and the use of the blues as signifying--are necessary considerations when evaluating the African American novel and, I believe, all have played a critical part in this work.

In Chapter One, I outline the general characteristics of the slave narrative: they are first-person accounts which emphasize the brutality of slavery, the cruel separation of family members, especially of children from their mothers, and the slave's lack of identity as a result of the break up the family, and other points. Because of the consistent treatment of similar themes in slave narratives and because of their political nature, reader expectations placed restraints on the depth to which authors could explore any one facet of slave life. The novel, therefore, provided the literary and thematic freedoms which slave narratives did not. William Wells Brown, who had written his own slave narrative, utilized the novel's artistic freedoms to fashion the novel *Clotel* as a way to focus on some of the other horrors slavery created, especially the fate of his novel's young heroines who fall victim to the laws of *femme coverte*. In this chapter, I am especially interested in responding to Werner Sollors' argument, presented in his work *Beyond Ethnicity*[14] that ethnic American literature often dramatized the new immigrant's dilemma of having to choose between traditional ethnic/blood loyalties and the personal freedoms which are part of America's typology. Sollors defines these as descent/consent choices, respectively. My response to Sollors in this chapter is that African American literature as it depicts slave life in *Clotel* and in Chesnutt's *The Conjure Woman* precludes the option of choice based on consent (free will) and, as a result, his arguments are not fully applicable to African American literature.

Chapter Two examines the good-mother tradition as a trope in African American literature. Harriet Jacobs' slave narrative *Incidents*, one of the few by a woman, helps establish the literary record of this tradition, which is characterized by self-sacrificing women who endure incredible hardships for the sake of their children.[15] This literary tradition, which is supported by a strong oral tradition, serves as a palimpsestic subtext for the characterizations of Ann Petry's Lutie Johnson in *The Street* and Alice Walker's Meridian Hill in *Meridian*. Petry's portrayal of life in Harlem is so naturalistic, however, that her heroine cannot survive both as a woman *and* a mother. In Alice

Walker's *Meridian*, her heroine discovers that, by rejecting her culturally assigned roles as a wife and mother, her struggle to redefine her role as a woman in society is not only painful, but requires a regeneration of spirit and renewed commitment to her race.

Chapter Three examines Walker's masterpiece, *The Color Purple*. I begin my discussion by comparing its social relevance as a model for redefining sexual and cultural roles to Hurston's *Their Eyes Were Watching God*.[16] Next, I show that it is part of Walker's plan to explore the fact that while folklore serves a number of functions in society, not all of them are good. Walker, in fact, creates characters and scenes which become retellings of specific folk tales collected by Hurston. Walker's rendering of these tales illustrates how elements of sexism and paternalism in folk tales are used by men to justify their domination and abuse of women, particularly Celie and Sofia. Finally, Walker's novel seeks to expose the limitations of folklore and, at the same time, to provide new models of living and cooperation between the sexes.

Chapter Four discusses Toni Morrison's *The Bluest Eye* in two lights. The first examines the theme of abandonment as dramatized by black male writers and compares it to Morrison's handling of the theme. Whereas the male writers frequently portray their alienated protagonists as avoiding conflict through flight and abandonment, Morrison provides, in the narrator Claudia, the counter-image of a young girl who is capable of self-definition and of providing strategies for living which do not require flight, or madness. This chapter's second half focuses on Morrison's use of the blues to define the cultural groundedness of her characters. This strategy provides new insight into the characterizations of Pauline and Cholly and their relative responsibility for Pecola's madness.

Chapter Five focuses on *Sula* and continues to examine Morrison's use of the blues. In this chapter, I utilize Houston Baker's *Blues, Ideology, and Afro-American Literature: A Vernacular Theory*,[17] and Ralph Ellison's definition of the blues to argue that Sula's improvisational nature makes her a tropological, numinous incarnation of the blues and as such she serves a vital role in the Bottom's existence. I also make extensive use of Henry Louis Gates' *Signifying Monkey*,[18] applying its theory of signifying, to discuss Sula's depiction as a signifier of the blues. This chapter looks at the role of improvisation in defining the blues and at Morrison's creative use of folk-tale and folk-legend conventions to define the Bottom. This chapter also argues that Sula's death, because she is a physical incarnation of the Bottom's folk heritage and because the members of the Bottom fear and reject her, prefigures the Bottom's demise.

A number of critical works form the framework for my discussion of the literature in this study. It is to these critical studies that I now turn as a way of making my own work more accessible.

In *Blues, Ideology, and Afro-American Literature: A Vernacular Theory*, Houston Baker proposes a theory of literary criticism which is discursive and profits by the examination and application of a number of ideologies.

Borrowing from Michel Foucault, Baker calls for an approach to the study of American literary history that embraces an "archaeology of knowledge." Baker explains: "As a method of analysis, the archaeology of knowledge assumes that knowledge exists in discursive formations whose lineage can be traced and whose regularities are discoverable. Hence, the mystery and sacrosanctness that often surround 'bodies of knowledge' or 'disciplines' are replaced, under the prospect of the archaeology of knowledge, by an acknowledgement of such bodies as linguistic constructs" (p. 17). As Baker further explains, "Foucault's concern to set his archaeology of knowledge in nonsubjective terms leads him to talk of statements and laws rather than of, say, speakers and intentions" (p. 18).

Discussing Roland Barthes' essay "Historical Discourse," Baker states that: "Barthes's formulation enables us to conceive of the governing statements of American history and evolutionary stages of American literary history as materially repeatable entities that assume the status of facts only because they are inscribed in historical discourse" (p. 22). Using the example of the discovery of an Iguanodon tooth, the importance and meaning of which changed through time as the science of paleontology developed, Baker makes this analogy: "Just as an enlarged context altered the conception of Iguanodon, so a consideration of the discursive constellation can alter our view of historical discourse. When the discourses and practices contemporary with American history are brought to bear, its religious orientation, site, and authorities are subject to radical reinterpretation" (p. 23).

Baker builds upon his representation of Foucoult and Barthes, arriving at the following point: "... what interests me is a form of thought that grounds Afro-American discourse in concrete, material situations. Where Afro-American narratives are concerned, the most suitable analytical model is not only an economic one, but also one based on a literary-critical frame of reference. The type of ideological model I have in mind is suggested by the scholarly reflections both of [Fredric] Jameson and of Hayden White, another well-known critic of dialectical thought" (pp. 25-6).

Then, following his brief discussion of Jameson and White, Baker says that to bring the positions of these two scholars together "is to gain a view of *subtextual dimensions* of Afro-American discourse that have never been effectively evaluated" (p.26, emphasis added). What Baker is driving toward, for African American literature, is a "shift from a 'traditional' to an economic perspective, from a humanistic to an ideologically oriented frame of reference, [which] evokes what might be called the 'economics of slavery'" (p. 26). The economics of slavery, Baker states: "stands as a governing statement in Afro-American discourse. In specifically Afro-American terms, the 'economics of slavery' signifies the social system of the Old South that determined what, how, and for whom goods were produced to satisfy human wants" (p. 26).

If we consider the economics of slavery as an essential component of the subtextual dimension of African American discourse, it is in the blues as trope that that economics resides as subtext. The role blues play as trope is of central importance to Baker's argument, and to this work. Baker defines the trope and its importance thus:

> Tropological thought is a discursive mode that employs unfamiliar (or exotic) figures to qualify what is deemed 'traditional' in a given discourse.... The end of tropological enterprise is the alteration of reality itself.... The process of tropological understanding is coextensive with dialectical thought. It, too, is designed to achieve an enlarged, altered, more adequate discursive rendering of the object of knowledge (pp. 28-29).

One way to achieve this shift in perspective is to view the blues as a matrix, a womb, a synthesis, an amalgam of work songs, proverbial wisdom, folk philosophy, and other folk expressions that "seems always to have been in motion in America--always becoming, shaping, transforming, displacing the peculiar experiences of Africans in the New World" (p. 5). As a trope, the blues matrix signify a history of economic deprivation, loss, hardship, and, at their root, the experience and legacy of slavery. A comprehension and understanding of the blues and their significance for African American literary study, is essential, therefore, to plumb these texts' tropological and subtextual meaning.

Baker cautions, however, that "it is not ... blues that provide a *first* occasion for examining the operation of 'economics of slavery' and 'commercial deportation' as governing statements of Afro-American discourse" (p. 31). Rather, that first view "is provided ... by African slave narratives." Not surprisingly though, slave narratives "reveal subtextual contours rich in 'blues resources'" (p. 31). Baker thus suggests that the blues, while implied or signified in early slave narrative, are not yet explicitly stated as such--they exist, instead, at the level of subtext.

Thus, while it is possible to recognize the blues subtext of slavery and oppression and to discern the economics of slavery in *Clotel* and *The Conjure Woman*, for example, and further to see in Uncle Julius the figure of an improvisational trickster, their respective authors do not label these characters, "blues" characters. I would claim that the blues manifest themselves in these early African American works in an inchoate stage, or a condition of liminality.[19] This is in contrast to more modern novels which often define characters specifically in terms of their "blues" characteristics--both Lutie Johnson and Shug Avery (of *The Street* and *The Color Purple*, respectively), for instance, are blues singers, a fact which signifies upon their character, and their status in the novel. That the blues remain subtextual in African American slave narratives speaks more to the thematic and humanizing exigencies of the narratives, than it does to the presence of the blues.

The blues defy simple definition; they signify more than a single definition can relate. Placing the blues in an ideological framework, Baker states that "the blues ... comprise a mediational site where familiar antinomies are resolved (or dissolved) in the office of adequate cultural understanding" (p. 6). True as that is, however, the blues matrix "avoids simple dualities" (p. 9). In Baker's terms, "the blues matrix defines itself as a network mediating poverty and abundance in much the same manner that it reconciles durative ['lyrical statements of injustice, despair, loss, absence, denial' (p. 7)] and kinetic" (p. 8).

Baker argues that in the early slave narratives of Olaudah Equino and Frederick Douglass these antinomic forces are "resolved" only when these writers are able to participate in and master mercantile enterprise, thereby achieving liberation (pp. 37-39). Furthermore, the literary record of these narratives, especially their subtextual discourse recounting their authors' successful mercantilism, build upon one another. As a result, African American texts possess a "palimpsestic character" (p. 39). This metaphor suggests that texts not only build upon one another, but also signify upon one another--thus close study of the early slave narratives frequently reveals the slave's understanding that in order to become free in capitalistic America, the economics of slavery demanded that the slave acquire the fiscal means to purchase his own freedom. Subsequent slave narratives provide a restatement or a reworking of that crucial enterprise. As Baker points out, in Frederick Douglass's narrative, Douglass discovers that "revolt, religion, and literacy *all* fail" (p. 47) to procure freedom for Douglass. What is required, is to acquire the means to buy freedom and to navigate the "economics of slavery."[20] Admittedly, Baker's text is so rich it is difficult to do justice to its insights in so brief a manner as this. This work focuses on those of Baker's insights and arguments which support its own particular claims--most especially: the blues are a trope which defy simple definition, yet which signify upon a history of oppression which is somehow transcended through the lyrical expression of the indomitable human spirit; Baker's recognition of the palimpsestic nature of African American texts; and the "economics of slavery" as subtext.

Henry Louis Gates's *The Signifying Monkey: A Theory of African-American Literary Criticism*, like Baker's study, reassesses the African American literary tradition in terms of the vernacular. Gates states: "*The Signifying Monkey* explores the relation of the black vernacular tradition to the Afro-American literary tradition. The book attempts to identify a theory of criticism that is inscribed within the black vernacular tradition and that in turn informs the shape of the Afro-American literary tradition" (p. xix). In the two trickster figures of Esu (Yoruban) and the Signifying Monkey (Afro-American), "two separate but related trickster figures," Gates discovers a "meta-discourse" in which these two figures "serve in their respective traditions as points of conscious articulation of language traditions aware of themselves as traditions, complete with a history, patterns of development and revision, and internal principles of patterning and organization" (pp. xx-xxi).

Gates' study shows Esu's mythological function as a messenger "who interprets the will of the gods to man" and as one who is by nature "double-voiced" (p. 6). Gates claims that the black tradition is itself double-voiced, and defines four types of double-voiced textual relations: *Tropological Revision, The Speakerly Text, Talking Texts,* and *Rewriting the Speakerly.*[21] From this tradition, "the Signifying Monkey emerges from his mysteriously beclouded Afro-American origins as Esu's first cousin, if not his American heir" (p. 20). It is this character, the Signifying Monkey, which serves "as the figure-of-figures, as the trope in which are encoded several other peculiarly black rhetorical tropes." Gates goes on to say that he is "concerned to demonstrate that the Monkey's language of Signifyin(g) functions as a metaphor for formal revision, or intertextuality, within the Afro-American literary tradition" (p. xxi).[22]

In one respect, Gates' critical approach is a restatement of Houston Baker's. What Gates defines as "intertextuality," Baker has described as "palimpsestic." Together, their arguments herald a discursive approach to African American literary study which emphasizes the value and integrity of vernacular speech, expression, and signification (which is double-voiced--saying one thing, while implying another via indirection). As Gates states: "Signifyin(g) is a black rhetorical difference that negotiates the language user through several orders of meaning" (p. 79). About African American writers whose works signify upon earlier texts, Gates claims: "This form of formal revision is what I am calling critical signification, or formal Signifyin(g), and is my metaphor for literary history" (p. 107).

For the jazz artist, improvisational reworkings may be less formal, more spontaneous. Still, it is from the improvisational nature of jazz that such formal attempts at literary revision may have evolved. As Gates states his thesis: "Improvisation, of course, so fundamental to the very idea of jazz is 'nothing more' than repetition and revision.... It is this principle of repetition and difference, this practice of intertextuality, which has been so crucial to the black vernacular forms of Signifyin(g), jazz--and even its antecedents, the blues, the spirituals, and ragtime--and which is the source of my trope for black intertextuality in the Afro-American formal literary tradition" (pp. 63-64).

Gates is careful to state that signifying "is a principle of language use and is not in any way the exclusive province of black people" (p. 90). Nor is the blackness of black literature "an absolute or a metaphysical condition.... Rather, the 'blackness' of black American literature can be discerned only through close readings. By 'blackness' here I mean specific uses of literary language that are shared, repeated, critiqued, and revised" (p. 121).

Gates claims (supported by evidence from Claudia Mitchell-Kernan) that Signifyin(g) is "a conscious rhetorical strategy" and this strategy is implicitly taught by black adults to their children. The result is that: "The mastery of Signifyin(g) creates *homo rhetoricus Africanus*, allowing--through the manipulation of these classic black figures of Signification--the black person to move freely between two discursive universes" (p. 75).

Like Houston Baker's *Blues, Ideology, and Afro-American Literature*, Gates' *The Signifying Monkey* is richly suggestive. Their exploration of black vernacular rhetorical strategies, formal and improvisational, intertextual and palimpsestic, serve as an exploration of what is unique about African American literature in our larger American literary canon. Certainly, an appreciation of African American literature's uniqueness underlies much of this work.

That sense of uniqueness does not, however, go so far as to view the black and white literatures of America as depictions of necessarily contrary cultural values, as proponents of Afrocentrism would have it. The tenets of Afrocentricity, which emerged by the early 1980s, have been espoused by M.K. Asante, N. Akbar, and others. The topic of Afrocentricity has gained so much attention that an entire issue of *Journal of Black Studies* was devoted to it.[23] As laudable as the goals of Afrocentricity are, especially as they strive to promote the unity and integrity of the African American family, an unfortunate bi-product of its agenda is the creation of a specious dichotomy or polarity, in which values that are not deemed worthwhile are labelled Eurocentric, or Euro-American (i.e., white). Thus, it is possible for scholars to report the following:

> The basic principles defining the Euro-American worldview are
> 'survival of the fittest' and 'control over nature' (people, objects,
> material possessions).... Consistent with Euro-American
> worldview, the values of power, competition, material
> affluence, and physical gratification (or pleasure) have been
> shown to govern heterosexual relationships in Euro-American
> society.... some researchers have shown that relationships in
> Euro-American culture are based on the principles of control
> and domination, or a hierarchy of power. The male is defined
> as the power-figure in such relationships. He is expected to be
> the dominant and controlling family member.... Overall, then,
> the evidence seems to strongly support the contention that
> heterosexual relationships in American society are heavily
> influenced by the Eurocentric cultural orientation emphasizing
> individualism, materialism, and physical gratification.[24]

(One gets the impression that Afrocentrists feel Europe invented
patriarchal societies; and that Afrocentrists have not read the literature
of Alice Walker, particularly *The Color Purple* and *Possessing the
Secret of Joy*.) By implication, "Euro-American" values are not suited
for culturally fit Afro-Americans. Conversely, "healthy Black
heterosexual relationships ... are governed by an "Afrocentric
imperative ... [meaning] the spiritual and intellectual commitment of
Black couples to the cultural affirmation of their people." The four
major components of that value system are: "sacrifice, inspiration,
vision, and victory."[25]

Regrettably, little or nothing is said that frames the existence
of these disparaged Euro-American values as being the result of
capitalism, class struggle, consumerism, or other historical, political,
and/or economic struggles. Nor does the Afrocentric position, as it is
presented in this particular issue of the *Journal of Black Studies*,
concede that millions of white Americans are oppressed and victimized
by the commercial forces of American society too.

The unfortunate offshoot of this battle of value systems, is its
entry into African American literary criticism. A recent article in the
African American Review discussed Gloria Naylor's novel *Mama Day*
is just such terms.[26] Value systems were polarized into white/black
(Euro-American/Afrocentric) values. Using this model, it was possible,
as the critic did, to simplistically criticize the character George for

spending his Sundays watching professional football, among other things, as proof of his seduction by "white" values, rather than as proof of his seduction by the forces of consumer economics and commercial advertising. To press my point: to condemn George for watching a "white man's game," is likewise to condemn hundreds of black professional football players, and thousands of amateurs, for playing it. I will not argue that George is culturally grounded, for he is not, and certainly the mass media has a lot to do with that, as the novel presents it. (In the novel, even Shakespeare is put to task.) But to call his failings the result of Euro-American values is too simplistic.

While acknowledging the need to discuss the unique differences that exist between the American and African American cultures, I find it disturbing that ideological debate over these value systems has created such fierce dichotomies while also suggesting that the acquisition of some white "American" or "Eurocentric" values by African Americans is paramount to cultural betrayal. There are no universal African American values, any more than there are universal African values or universal American values.

I address this uneasy debate here not only because I find it specious, but because this study has often found it necessary to discuss certain works, Toni Morrison's *The Bluest Eye* and *Sula*, for instance, utilizing a critical stance which recognizes that in fictive works, African American authors often portray black characters in terms of their cultural groundedness or uprootedness: ie., their connection to black African American values versus their connection to white American values. While I have found it necessary to discuss these fictive themes in a way that recognizes the insidious nature of certain "white" values, I have tried to avoid absolute (Afrocentric) polarizations in my discussion. Thus, while in *The Bluest Eye* I recognize that Pauline and Pecola are victimized and seduced by a "white" value system, it must also be said, extratextually, that many white Americans are also victimized by mass media (economic and political) attempts to define what beauty is (and any number of other values and opinions). Any one who lives in America is subject to the same forces, the same predations of mass-marketing and economic exploitation--not just racial minorities, although minorities may suffer from these forces more acutely.

Therefore, in discussing the term "white," this work is not suggesting, or agreeing with the Afrocentric notion that such a value system in fact represents the values embraced by the majority of "white"

Americans. What is meant by a "white" value system are those social, political, and economic tastes, fashions, and values which capitalism and popular culture promulgate and which continue to demean, delimit, and relegate to the margins the contributions, talents, and existence of African Americans in a larger white-dominated society.

In this work, I engage a series of arguments which recognize both the uniqueness of African American literature as well as the similarities it has with other literature, especially thematically. With this in mind, I embrace critical efforts which attempt to illustrate the common humanity and concerns of those peoples who have come to America and made it their home. A recent critical effort has attempted to do just that: to illustrate the similarities common to all types of "immigrant" literature, a category which includes African American literature.

In the introductory chapter to his book *Beyond Ethnicity,* Werner Sollors confronts this issue and argues that American literature should not be seen as a collection of unique and dissimilar literatures. Instead, Sollors pleads for a more unified vision, one which stresses the common experiences and dilemmas inherent in the process of acculturation and amalgamation which every immigrant faces in his struggle to redefine allegiances in a New Land. American-ethnic literature, Sollors contends, bears a number of striking and unifying similarities, particularly in the depiction of the new immigrants' struggle to resolve the tensions which exist between their ethnic past and their American future. Sollors states:

> This tension between the rejection of hereditary old-world
> hierarchies (embodied by the European nobility) and the vision
> of a new people of diverse nativities united in the fair pursuit
> of happiness marks the course that American ideology has
> steered between descent and consent. It is this conflict which
> is at the root of the ambiguity surrounding the very
> terminology of American ethnic interaction.[27]

Sollors adds: "definitions of American identity--between *consent* and *descent*--[are] the central drama in American culture" (p. 6). Sollors defines the terms descent and consent as: "Descent relations are those defined by anthropologists as relations of 'substance' (by blood or nature); consent relations describe those of 'law' or 'marriage'" (p. 6). He further claims that "Works of ethnic literature ... may thus be read not only as expressions of mediation between cultures but also as handbooks of socialization into the codes of Americanness" (p. 7).

Sollors' fear is that literary histories of the United States will deal with ethnic groups in "random essays" [as has the 1988 edition of the *Columbia Literary History of the United States*], instead of discussing, or attempting to discover, the common ground and issues upon which all American literature is based. *Beyond Ethnicity* thus attempts to uncover those common themes; one prominent example being the typological vision of America as a New Eden in which immigrants, as the new Chosen People, hopefully find a new life. Sollors' position can be summarized as:

> If anything, ethnic literary history ought to *increase* our understanding of the cultural interplays and contacts among writers of different backgrounds, the cultural mergers and secessions that took place in America, all of which can be accomplished only if the categorization of writers as members of ethnic groups is understood to be a very partial, temporal, and insufficient characterization at best (pp. 14-15).

With good reason, Sollors appears acutely sensitive to the nature of African American literature and the contention that black literature is not just ethnic but also *racial*. Sollors' sensitivity to this problem surfaces in the very first chapter (pp. 36-39). When Sollors opts to place the issue of race under the jurisdiction of ethnicity, he adds that his decision is not "an attempt to gloss over the special legacy of slavery and racism in America" (p. 37). Sollors concedes that slavery "contradicts ... many of [the] generalizations of American life" (p. 37); he further concedes that this issue is particularly prickly because "this supposedly consent-focused culture [America] also *produced*--not inherited--segregation, one of the most sharply formulated systems of descent-based discrimination in the nineteenth and twentieth centuries" (p. 37).

Later, in his comparative study of Chesnutt's "The Wife of His Youth" (1898) and Cahan's *Yekl* (1896), Sollors stresses the striking and numerous plot similarities of these ethnically diverse stories (black and Jewish)--while down playing the stories' divergent and antithetical resolutions, which Sollors argues, are the "right" conclusions to stories written in different ways ("Wife" as romance, *Yekl* as realism) (pp. 149-73).

While I find Sollors' work instructive and valuable, it is the contention of, most especially, this study's first chapter that the differences in resolution run deeper than the correctness of differing literary conventions. Chesnutt is but one of many black writers in a white society who saw little hope for integration in a racist society. Issues of consent/descent were not for black writers, as they were for other ethnic writers, true alternatives. The blacks' fate has been and continues to be *mandated* along race lines (that is, descent lines) because in fact the dominant white culture has not yet consented to racial equality between blacks and whites. So, while Sollors' scheme has relevance to other ethnic groups in America, and *limited* application to blacks in specific instances, as a general rule, blacks cannot be seen as falling into the American literary melting pot. My conclusion is not based solely, or even primarily, on Sollors' discussion. Instead, it stems from a historical perspective which cannot be easily argued away. When John Henrik Clarke claims: "in the cry for black power and black history, black people are saying a very powerful, complex, yet simple thing: 'I am a man,'" he is echoing the voice of other blacks, not a few of whom did not live in this century. When Clarke states that "The family, the most meaningful entity in African life, was systematically destroyed" by slavery, and that "The greatest destroyer of African culture ... was the plantation system of the New World," and that nowhere in the Americas was the repression and destruction of African culture as thorough as in the United States, Clarke is also implying that the black-American experience in the United States is unique and without parallel.[28] Certainly black Americans aspired to be free, and cradled the dream of democracy within their hearts as all "immigrants" have done. But the writings of no other people are so preoccupied with proving the fundamental premise that "I am a man," that I am human, as is black literature. That is a voice that knows no equal.

I bring up Sollors in detail to argue for the *specific* differences of African Americans from other ethnics, and for its unique position in American literature. Certainly, suffering, patriarchy, political oppression, and even slavery itself, are universal experiences, and world literature is full of examples. But African American literature has its own unique concerns, its own history, its own voice, and its own language.

When Toni Morrison asks "what constitutes the art of a black writer.... In other words, other than melanin and subject matter, what, in fact, may make me a black writer? Other than my own ethnicity-- what is going on in my work that makes me believe it is demonstrably inseparable from a cultural specificity that is Afro-American?"[29] she asks a legitimate question, the very question I am asking here. Morrison offered an answer to her own question, earlier in the same essay:

> What makes a work "Black"? The most valuable point of entry into the question of cultural (or racial) distinction, the one most fraught, is its language--its unpoliced, seditious, confrontational, manipulative, inventive, disruptive, masked and unmasking language. Such a penetration will entail the most careful study, one in which the impact of Afro-American presence on modernity becomes clear and is no longer a well-kept secret.[30]

Houston Baker has also suggested that the sui generis quality of African American literature is its language:

> Culture, in my operative definition, is analogous to linguistic discourse. A linguistic discourse is a structure consisting of language units higher than or "beyond" the sentence, i.e., two conjoined sentences, a myth, a folktale, a novel, and so on....
> ...individuals who enter a culture where the language is unfamiliar may be capable (after a relatively brief period) of identifying and defining in their own terms any single word or sentence presented, and they may rapidly become adept at constructing interesting ethnographic accounts for their "home" cultures. But they will not comprehend the overall game of language, or the culture's composite of language games, until they have fully grasped the general rules and procedures of discourse operating within the culture. Their understanding will remain tenuous until they have engaged in the process that the symbolic anthropologist Clifford Geertz calls "thick description."[31]

African American literature does have its own language, its own signifiers, as has already been pointed out. At the same time, while this work is not in full agreement with Werner Sollors' *Beyond Ethnicity*, it does appreciate his efforts to discover the common ground, the common blood that makes all of America's literatures, American literature.

I conclude this introduction with a quote from Houston Baker's *The Journey Back*, and trust that this study will provide the kind of valuable insight that Baker claims is essential to fully appreciate African American literature.

But if black creativity is the result of a context--of webs of meaning--different in kind and degree from those conceived within the narrow attitudinal categories of white America, it seems possible that the semantic force of black creativity might escape the white critic altogether. And where black American works of literature and verbal art are involved, a case can certainly be made for the cultural specificity of meaning. The argument involved, however, requires an open, analytical mind on the part of both the investigator and his audience. But it is worth pursuing if one is interested in comprehending not only the expressive manifestations of black America, but also some additional reasons for the white commentator's ofttimes superficial accounts of black verbal art....

No analyst can understand the black literary text who is not conscious of the semantic levels of black culture. The journey to this level is by way of the whole discourse comprising black American culture.[32]

NOTES

1. *Clotel; or The President's Daughter [with a Sketch of the Author's Life]* (New York: Citadel Press, 1969).

2. William Edward Farrison, "Introduction to *Clotel*," Ibid., p. 7.

3. (Ann Arbor: University of Michigan Press, 1969).

4. Alice Walker, *Meridian* (New York: Pocket Books, 1986); *The Color Purple* (New York: Harcourt Brace Jovanovich, Publishers, 1982); Toni Morrison, *The Bluest Eye* (New York: Washington Square Press, 1972); *Sula* (New York: Plume, 1982).

5. Harriet Jacobs, *Incidents in the Life of a Slave Girl* (New York: Harcourt Brace Jovanovich, Publishers, 1973); Ann Petry, *The Street* (Boston: Beacon Press, 1985).

6. To claim that most earlier African American writers were writing primarily for white audiences is a broad claim, certainly. And to suggest that the endpoint of this period is the middle of the twentieth century is debatable. Nonetheless, it seems generally correct. One point that is germane to this claim is the literacy rate among African Americans, up until the turn of the century. In *The Souls of Black Folk*, DuBois claimed of one representative county in Georgia, the state he claimed had more blacks than any other in the Union at that time that: "The degree of ignorance cannot easily be expressed. We may see, for instance, that nearly two-thirds of them [blacks] cannot read or write" (in *Three Negro Classics* [New York: Avon Books, 1965], pp. 185, 307.) This says something about who African Americans *could* reach with their writings.

The claim that earlier African American writers copied the literary models (forms) of their white audiences, refers to Phillis Wheatley's imitation of British poets, especially Alexander Pope and Thomas Grey. It refers also to Harriet Jacobs' use of sentimentality and her deference to decorum in her slave-narrative *Incidents in the Life of a Slave Girl* (1861). Charles Chesnutt's use of the conventions of the historical romance as practiced by Walter Scott are evident in his novel *The House Behind the Cedars* (1900).

The intent of earlier African American works also speaks to my general point. Wilson Moses reminds us that "the slave narrative [was] propaganda." Furthermore, as propaganda, the authors (and the publishers) of slave narratives were keenly aware of their intended audience:

> Black males who wrote slave narratives were fully aware that their audience was made up of evangelical Christians. The ultimate foundation of abolitionist morality was based on the idea that slavery was an assault on the nuclear family and the sacred place of the woman within the home. Abolitionist audiences wanted to be told that slavery destroyed households and corrupted sexual morality... ("Writing Freely?: Frederick Douglass and the Constraints of Racialized Writing" in *Frederick Douglass: New Literary and Historical Essays*, ed., Eric J. Sundquist [Cambridge: Cambridge University Press, 1990], p. 71).

Robert Bone, in his work *The Negro Novel in America* provides evidence that black writers--an obvious portion of the Talented Tenth--during the period of 1890-1920 were writing both for themselves (meaning other members of the Talented Tenth) and for white audiences. Their writings had two goals--one "inspirational," the other "protest" ([New Haven, CT: Yale University Press, 1958], p. 15).

In 1928, James Weldon Johnson wrote about the special dilemma facing the black writer when envisioning his audience: "...the Aframerican [sic] author faces a special problem which the plain American author knows nothing about--the problem of the double audience. It is more than a double audience; it is a divided audience, an audience made up of two elements with differing points of view. His audience is always both white America and black America" ("The Dilemma of the Negro Author," *The American Mercury*, Dec. 1928: p. 477).

James Baldwin's *The Fire Next Time* (1962), despite its artifice of being a letter of his nephew, serves as a warning to white America. And it would be prudent to keep in mind a sense of proportion when, as Albert Murray argues in *The Omni-American* (1970), we come to a text like Claude Brown's *Manchild in the Promised Land* (1965). Murray's harsh criticism of Brown's novel is based upon the media's "positive" response to the work because, Murray believes, it serves up a portrait of Harlem that the media thinks typifies the black experience. Murray writes:

> As a matter of fact *Manchild* (a title that probably makes some white people think they know how chitterlings and collard greens taste), like so many other books written for white people by Negroes, is so full of the fashionable assumptions of the social sciences that little of what its young author has to reveal about what it is like to be one very special Harlem Negro named Claude Brown really represents his own insights ([New York: Outerbridge & Dienstfrey, 1970], pp. 98-99).

In toto, these arguments present a complex picture of the forces which contribute to the question of who the African American writer's intended audience is. Time, race, and politics each play a part. In summary, it would be well to keep in mind the special needs of certain texts when assessing them critically.

    7. Wilson Moses claimed that Frederick Douglass' *Narrative*, while sincere and honest, was nonetheless subject to certain demands: "If writing freely means writing not only abundantly, but with absolute or impolitic condor, Douglass did not write freely of himself. Douglass' literary act of self-presentation was skillfully engineered to produce desired effects on certain sets of white liberals." Furthermore, William Lloyd Garrison had pressured Douglass to fit a certain stereotypic mold in his public oratory and in his later writings, as well. Moses writes: "Douglass's later oratory and writing celebrated not only a struggle against the reactionaries of the slave power but also a victory over the abolitionists who encouraged him to speak substandard English (slave vernacular) and discouraged him from starting his own newspaper. No version of the narrative [there were four] dwells in detail on Douglass's philosophical objections to Garrisonian tactics. Perhaps he felt compelled to pull his punches when it came to public criticism of white liberals" ("Writing Freely?: Frederick Douglass and the Constraints of Racialized Writing, in *"Frederick Douglass: New Literary and Historical Essays,* Ibid., p. 68, p. 76).

    8. (Bloomington: Indiana University Press, 1978), p. 4.

9. *The Souls of Black Folk*, Ibid., p. 215.

10. *Shadow and Act* (New York: Vintage Books, 1972), p. xxi.

11. (Chicago: University of Chicago Press, 1980), p. 108.

12. *Blues People: The Negro Experience in White America and the Music That Developed From It* (New York: Morrow Quill Paperbacks, 1963), p. 95.

13. Gene Bluestein has studied Ralph Ellison's use of the blues in *Invisible Man* (*The Voice of the Folk*, [Amherst, CT: Yale University Press, 1958], pp. 117-40). And Albert Murray has argued that the blues, as an existential philosophy which emphasizes "an affirmative and hence exemplary and heroic response to that which Andre Malraux describes as *la condition humaine*," has a place in the political behavior of African Americans as well (*The Omni-Americans: New Perspectives on Black Experience and American Culture* [New York: Outerbridge & Dienstfrey, 1970], pp. 58-61).

14. *Beyond Ethnicity: Consent and Descent in American Culture* (New York: Oxford University Press, 1986).

15. Langston Hughes' poem "The Negro Mother" is another literary effort which valorizes black motherhood. See *Selected Poems of Langston Hughes* (New York: Vintage Books, 1974), pp. 288-89.

16. Zora Neale Hurston, *Their Eyes Were Watching God* (Greenwich, CT: Fawcett Publications, 1965).

17. *Blues, Ideology, and Afro-American Literature* (Chicago: The University of Chicago Press, 1984). All citations of Baker's work refer to this edition and are hereafter marked by page numbers in parentheses.

18. *The Signifying Monkey: A Theory of African-American Criticism* (New York: Oxford University Press, 1988). All citations refer to this edition and are denoted in parentheses.

19. I am borrowing the term liminality from Houston Baker's *Blues, Ideology*. His usage deals with rites of passage, but seems analogous here. The definition he provides is this: "'liminality'--that 'betwixt and between' phase of rites of passage when an individual has left one fixed social status but has not yet been incorporated into another" (p. 183).

20. This point is rich with possibilities for a re-estimation of the old quarrel between Booker T. Washington's argument for the necessity of trade school's versus W.E.B. DuBois' championing of liberal education. To wit: Both Houston Baker and Henry Louis Gates

agree that the slave narrative represents the beginnings of African American literature: Baker says "The locus classicus of Afro-American literary discourse is the slave narrative"; Gates says "it is to the literature of the black slave that the critic must turn to identify the beginning of the Afro-American literary tradition" (*Blues, Ideology,* Ibid., p. 31; *The Signifying Monkey: A Theory of African-American Literary Criticism* [New York: Oxford University Press, 1988], p. 127.) Baker's emphasis is economics based, however, and thus appears to support Washington's argument for trade schools, whereas Gates' explication of the trope of the talking book suggests that literacy is the first thing slaves needed to acquire in their quest for freedom, thereby supporting DuBois' argument for liberal education.

21. Gates defines these terms thus: Tropological Revision: "the manner in which a specific trope is repeated, with differences, between two or more texts"; The Speakerly Text: "... is exemplified in the peculiar play of 'voices' at work in the use of 'free indirect discourse' in Zora Neale Hurston's *Their Eyes Were Watching God....* Free indirect discourse is represented in this canonical text as if it were a dynamic character, with shifts in its level of diction drawn upon to reflect a certain development of self-consciousness in a hybrid character, a character who is neither the novel's protagonist nor the text's embodied narrator, but a blend of both, an emerging and merging moment of consciousness."; Talking Texts: "a black form of intertextuality"; Rewriting the Speakerly: "If Hurston's novel [*Their Eyes*] seems to have been designed to declare that, indeed, a text could be written in black dialect.... [Alice] Walker ... revises and echoes Hurston in a number of ways [in *The Color Purple*]" (pp. xxv-xxvi).

22. Gates' presentation of the word "Signifyin(g)," as opposed to "signifying," is meant to suggest the linguistic, rhetorical, and cultural differences that language and actions imply for African Americans versus white-Americans, respectively. Gates states that: "Whereas signification depends for order and coherence on the exclusion of unconscious associations which any given word yields at any given time, Signification luxuriates in the inclusion of the free play of these associative rhetorical and semantic relations" (p. 49).

23. *Journal of Black Studies*, 21, no.2 (December 1990).

24. Yvonne R. Bell, Cathy L. Bouie, and Joseph A. Baldwin, "Afrocentric Cultural Consciousness and African-American Male-Female Relationships," Ibid., pp. 163-65.

25. Ibid.: p. 170.

26. Susan Meisenhelder, "'The Whole Picture' in Gloria Naylor's *Mama Day*," *African American Review* 27, no. 3 (Fall 1993): pp. 405-19.

27. *Beyond Ethnicity*, Ibid., pp. 4-5. All citations to this text which follow are to this edition and denoted by number in parentheses.

28. "Black Americans: Immigrants Against Their Will," *The Immigrant Experience in America*, ed. Frank J. Coppa and Thomas J. Curran (Boston: Twayne Publishers, 1976): pp. 186, 179, 178.

29. "Unspeakable Things Unspoken: Afro-American Presence in American Literature," *Modern Critical Views: Toni Morrison*, ed. Harold Bloom (New York: Chelsea House Publishing, 1990): p. 217.

30. Ibid., p. 210.

31. *The Journey Back* (Chicago: University of Chicago Press, 1980), pp. xiii-xiv.

32. Ibid., p. 154, p. 163.

Identity, Family, and Folklore in African American Literature

I

THE BLACK FAMILY IN NINETEENTH CENTURY
AFRICAN AMERICAN LITERATURE

When W. E. B. DuBois proclaimed that "the problem of the twentieth century is the problem of the color line" he was not only looking forward, but backwards.[1] Slavery and its legacy had left an indelible imprint on the nation, and on its literature. African American writers were especially attuned to the need to make white readers recognize the humanity of the black man and the sanctity of the black family. The Civil War and Emancipation, regrettably, did not bury the old prejudices and as a result the need for writers to explore and express the black man's humanity and love of family continued as an important theme.

The fact that a Christian country founded and predicated on the democratic ideals of consent would systematically and legally engage in slave trading and chattel slavery (and even after "emancipation" would continue in its courts to deny blacks equality) was not lost on the authors of slave narratives. The democratic and religious hypocrisy of Southern and Northern Americans, not just slave owners, was thus one of the principle targets of Frederick Douglass' *Narrative* (1845), William Wells Brown's *Sketch* (1846), and of the first African-American novel, William Wells Brown's *Clotel* (1853).[2]

Because the slave narratives had common objectives and were intended for a common audience, it is not surprising that they contained similar episodes recounting the ubiquitous atrocities of slavery. In a chapter from his work, *William Wells Brown and "Clotel,"* J. Noel Heermance has outlined the common characteristics of the slave narrative genre. These characteristics include: 1) a realistic portrayal of

3

slavery and its evils from a first person, eye-witness point of view; 2) portrayal of the early and brutal separation of children from their mothers; 3) the slaves' lack of identity, be it through dispersal or ignorance of family members, or having no surname, or both; 4) a recognition that the majority of fugitive slaves were mulattoes; and 5) the frequent use of anti-democratic and anti-Christian ironies.[3]

As Heermance makes clear, there are a number of thematic similarities inherent in slave narratives. One way to graphically illustrate one of those themes, the evils of slavery, was for the narratives to include a description of a lynching. Frederick Douglass' *Narrative* is no exception. In it, Douglass describes the murder of a slave who, having taken refuge in a creek, is given three warnings to come out, refuses, and is then summarily shot and killed (pp. 39-40).

The separation of mothers and children was another theme stressed in slave narratives. Douglass wrote: "my mother and I were separated when I was but an infant.... For what this separation is done, I do not know, unless it be to hinder the development of the child's affection toward its mother, and to blunt and destroy the natural affection of the mother for the child" (p. 22). Despite certain punishment if caught, Douglass recounts that his mother journeyed after a full day's work "to see me in the night, travelling the whole distance on foot" (p. 22).

William Wells Brown similarly recounts in his *Sketch* that he too was separated from his mother "at an early age" (p. 18); and at the age of ten, he found himself helpless to intervene when he heard his mother being whipped (p. 18). After some years, the narrative states, the pair were moved to Missouri. There, Brown convinced his mother to escape with him because "he loved his mother so intensely that he could not think of leaving without her" (p. 26). When their attempted flight for freedom failed, Brown's mother was sold, and he never saw her again.

Again, Frederick Douglass' fate was similar. He recounts seeing his brother brutally beaten by a slave owner: "[Master Andrew] took my little brother by the throat, threw him on the ground, and with the heel of his boot stamped upon his head till the blood gushed from his nose and ears..." (pp. 60-61). Surprisingly, Douglass states that in the face of such torture, the death of an owner, even a cruel one, would not necessarily make the slaves happy, for the specter of being sold off and separated from family members always loomed heavily in the slaves' minds, as his narrative makes clear: "A single word from the white men was enough--against all our wishes, prayers, and entreaties--to sunder forever the dearest friends, dearest kindred, and strongest ties known to human beings" (p. 60).

These examples taken from slave narratives, amply illustrate the horrors of slavery. When Brown wrote his novel, *Clotel*, he was free to borrow from the conventions of that genre. But Brown was also free to avoid the restraints implicit in slave narratives--especially the broad range of thematic concerns. By writing a novel about slavery, instead of a slave narrative, Brown was free to amplify one theme of signal importance: the break up of a family. In *Clotel*, the curse of Ham could serve as the signal underpinning of the novel, allowing Brown to focus upon the tragic fates of his "blood tainted" female characters, Currer, her daughters, and granddaughter, all of whom are ensnared, over the course of the novel, in the net of slavery. Brown believed in the sanctity of marriage and the sanctity of the family, and used his novel to make his white audience understand how important family bonds were to himself, and to his fellow blacks. Richard Lewis has said that Brown had an "intense regard for the family unit as an institution."[4] As the narrator of *Clotel*, Brown's own convictions speak for themselves:

Marriage is, indeed, the first and most important institution of human existence--the foundation of all civilization [sic] and culture--the root of church and state. It is the most intimate covenant of heart formed among mankind:.... It gives scope to every human virtue.... It unites all which ennobles and beautifies life.... it is the first and last sanctuary of human culture. As husband and wife, through each other become conscious of complete humanity, and every human feeling, and every human virtue; so children, at their first awakening in the fond covenant of love between parents, both of whom are tenderly concerned for the same object, find an image of complete humanity leagued in free love. The spirit of love which prevails between them acts with creative power upon the young mind, and awakens every germ of goodness within it.... If this be a true picture of the vast influence for good of the institution of marriage, what must be the moral degradation of that people to whom marriage is denied? (pp. 61-62)

In that novel, only a few pages after Brown's eloquent plea, Currer, the alleged slave-mistress of President Thomas Jefferson, and her daughters, Clotel and Althesa, are put up for sale. Clotel is sold and enslaved for one year, then escapes north disguised as a sickly white man, leaving behind her daughter, Mary. Currer and Althesa were also sold. The pair are bought by the same slave trader, Dick Miller, but they are not destined to remain together long, their fates resembling that of other slaves: "Husbands and wives were separated with a degree of indifference that is unknown in any other relation of life, except that of slavery" (p. 65). When Currer arrives in Natchez, Mississippi, she is inspected for purchase; at that time, she pleads with her future owner: "'If you buy me, I hope you will buy my daughter too'....." The owner's response is predictably callous: "'I only want one for my own use, and would not need another'" (p. 76).

The family is now torn apart, but familial bonds are not severed. Althesa is bought by James Crawford, a Vermonter who does not believe in slavery. They return north where Crawford sells Althesa to Henry Morton, a physician and boarder of Crawford's. Althesa and Morton marry, but Morton fails to manumit his wife. Althesa now tries to purchase her mother out of slavery, but fails. Clotel, after she has found freedom in Ohio as a runaway, risks her life to save her daughter, Mary, only to be captured and drowned "within plain sight of the President's [Jefferson] house and the capital of the Union" (p. 219).

The break up of Currer's family wasn't Brown's only object; he also uses his novel to track the individual destinies of each of *Clotel's* women. After Clotel drowns, Mary's fate is documented: she is sold to New Orleans, is saved by a Frenchman, Mr. Devenant; then she goes to France. Brown then turns to Althesa, and her daughters, Ellen and Jane. In them, Brown masterfully utilized the convention of the "tragic octoroon."

The convention of the "tragic octoroon," which Richard Lewis has called "more American than European,"[5] presented a heroine of mixed blood and therefore of mixed cultures, and played more than any other device on the fears of its white audience. Brown describes the beauty of *Clotel's* "tragic octoroons"--Clotel, Althesa, Ellen, and Jane--in terms meant to imitate the white Western ideal. These characterizations illustrate how difficult the color line can be to discern, and that, in some cases, given bizarre twists of fate, a woman sold as a black slave could, in fact, be white. Brown dramatizes that point in the novel by presenting the character Salome Miller, a German immigrant who is sold into slavery. Her story is told in Chapter xiv, aptly titled: "A FREE WOMAN REDUCED TO SLAVERY." The emotional impact of using the "tragic octoroon" convention was strong and personal, a point which Lewis, in his comments on the convention, did not overlook: "This strategy involves transference between the physical appearance of these tragic octoroons and the concept of ideal beauty in the Western world, i.e., the tragic octoroon serves as a literary mirror in which the white reading audience sees itself and its own children."[6] (Frederick Douglass seems to have adapted this convention when he described Aunt Hester's beauty in terms meant to rival a white woman's, and then shows her brutally beaten (pp. 25-26).)

Brown's *Clotel* dramatizes the tragic octoroon convention exceedingly well: because Althesa had never been manumitted by her husband, Morton, and was still a slave, her daughters, Ellen and Jane, aged 17 and 15 respectively, have no knowledge of their tenuous condition: i.e., that they too are slaves. We are told that the two girls "had never heard that their mother had been a slave, and therefore knew nothing of the danger hanging over their heads" (p. 207). Only after Althesa and her husband die of Yellow Fever do their daughters suddenly discover that they are, legally, slaves, like their mother. But by then, having been raised as white, lacking any knowledge of their black blood, the daughters have lived their lives ruled by consent relationships, especially in the realm of love. As a result, after the girls are sold into slavery, Ellen poisons herself rather than be abused sexually by the "old gentleman" who has purchased her for $2,300. Similarly, after Jane is bought for $3,000 by a young profligate "planter," she foresees her own sexual violation. After she is "locked up ... in her master's mansion" (true to the tragic octoroon convention) her boy friend, Volney Lapuc, a white medical student, attempts to rescue her, only to be shot and killed. Melodramatically, Jane dies of a "broken heart."

In *Clotel*, two "tragic octoroons," Ellen and Jane, die as a result of Morton's ignorance of Southern law: a law which proclaims that "children follow the condition of their mother" (p. 206). Brown dramatized these two senseless deaths to make two points. The first is that Morton's "ignorance"--or any Northerner's--is not an excuse for allowing the system of slavery to continue. The second point is more subtle: Can it be anything but self-serving hypocrisy for a nation which

functions under the principles and laws of *femme coverte*, and which is
paternalistic in both its legal and religious affairs to, in the case of
slavery, contend that maternal origin should determine a child's fate?
How is it that "children follow the condition of the mother" when white
women still did not have legal claims to their children?[7] The obvious
answer has been rendered by Frederick Douglass: "this is done too
obviously to administer to their [the slave owners'] own lusts, and make
a gratification of their wicked desires profitable as well as pleasurable."[8]

Of all the women only Mary escapes the fate of slavery.
Significantly, her haven is not in the hypocritical north, but France. And
her final happiness comes with a man, George Green, whom she had
loved earlier in her life and had helped escape from slavery. He too had
tried to purchase freedom for the one he loved, Mary, but had failed.
Only by accident are the two reunited after both came to find their
individual freedom in Europe.

Clotel, forged in the tradition of the slave narrative was, as a
novel, better suited to focus on the specific problems of love
relationships suffered under slavery. Slave narratives by their very
nature encompassed long passages of flight, and often detailed the
author's struggles to acquire an education; thus, while the systematic
destruction of family life was one of their focuses, it could be only one.
Clotel, on the other hand, as a novel was free to criticize all of slavery's
offenses, while focusing primarily on the struggles of black families to
keep their families together. In terms of consent/descent, Brown's *Clotel*
offers no hope that antebellum American would ever welcome the black
man as an equal partner--the nature of slavery demanded that black
descent, the curse of Ham, preclude issues of consent.

The gradual transference of allegiances from home country to
America, or the gradual realization that one could have both an
immediate family and be part of the greater American family, were
realizations summarily denied to all blacks. And while the shores of
America might have represented a rebirth, a New Eden, for European
immigrants, the American experience for blacks was more likely to be
chronicled as a series of deaths, as in *Clotel*. The ultimate rejection of
the American dream for those who escaped slavery was to live abroad:
for those "expatriates" the watery waves of baptism broke on the shores
of Europe.

Problems of "the color line" did not disappear with the abolition of slavery, nor did the need for black authors to insist, in their literature, that African Americans were loving and passionate human beings. The fiction of Charles Waddell Chesnutt, which followed Brown's by more than forty years, remained preoccupied with illustrating the humanity of blacks and the depth of their familial devotion. Two of Chesnutt's works, the short story "The Wife of His Youth," and the novel *The Conjure Woman*,[9] will now be examined to illustrate this point. These two works will also by discussed in light of Werner Sollors' *Beyond Ethnicity*,[10] a work which strives to illustrate the similarities inherent in the literature of new immigrants to America.

The first thing that excites the reader about Chesnutt's short story, "The Wife of His Youth" (1898) is the literary antecedents it suggests in its portrayals of its two central protagonists, Ryder and Liza Jane. Ryder is a light-skinned black who has gone to Washington, D.C., and quickly climbs the social ladder. His new life and success seems secure until the wife of his youth, Liza Jane, shows up to reclaim him for herself. Chesnutt's depiction of Ryder as a social outsider turned insider is intriguing because Ryder is able, by verve and energy, to become the "recognized adviser and head" (p. 3) of the Blue Veins. He foreshadows Zora Neale Hurston's Jody Starks who, in *Their Eyes Were Watching God* (1937), goes to Eatonville, Florida, and single-handedly fashions a town around its less energetic inhabitants. In Liza Jane, Chesnutt has foreshadowed Faulkner's Lena in *Light in August* (1932), each woman the wandering earth-mother seeking her husband.

Werner Sollors discusses this tale in *Beyond Ethnicity* in terms of its romantic qualities. Its structure, he argues, requires that Ryder choose Liza Jane over Molly Dixon, Ryder's new love: "In terms of romance, this is the only 'right' answer" (161). As convincing as Sollors is, he ignores other details of the story which perhaps suggested themselves to Chesnutt, himself a mulatto who chose not to pass as a white.[11]

The first detail of the story Sollors overlooks is that Mrs. Dixon "had come to Groveland from Washington"; she was also "much younger that he [Ryder]" (5). In these two details alone, Chesnutt suggests that Dixon symbolically represents both the promise of political freedom (consent), and the promise of rebirth and rejuvenation in the promised land of that freedom (consent). The problem is that neither aspiration was truly within the grasp of the American black at that time.

In his essay "Black Americans: Immigrants Against Their Will," John Clarke calls the period from 1877 to 1901 the "nadir" in Afro-American history: "This is the period when blacks lost the right to participate in the government of this country. During this period lynching became common and most of the Jim Crow laws also came into being."[12] Less a story concerned with real choices of descent/consent, "The Wife of His Youth" is an allegorical protest aimed at the lack of political choices and freedoms in America for blacks. Ryder's own sentiments support this reading:

> ...we people of mixed blood are ground between the upper and the nether millstone. Our fate lies between absorption by the white race and extinction in the black. The one doesn't want us yet, but may take us in time. The other would welcome us, but it would be for us a backward step. "With malice towards none, with charity for all," we must do the best we can for ourselves and those who are to follow us. (p. 7)

We might add to this Liza Jane's recollection that even as a free man, Sam [Ryder] was nearly sold into slavery (12). Chesnutt's conclusion is that in the American political scene, there was no real choice between consent/descent, only the guise. And just as Sam [Ryder] could once have been sold down the river, he could also, by marrying Mrs. Dixon, have found himself sold a bag of goods. Finally, there is the persistent theme, the strength of love bonds, which in this story does not represent a "backward step," but a realistic (not romantic) commitment to his race. This humanizes Ryder, by once again bonding him to the wife of his youth.

The Conjure Woman (1899) stands at the cusp of the nineteenth and twentieth centuries. And although *The Conjure Woman* appeared during, for blacks, the "nadir" of that political and cultural history, in a number of significant ways, this novel provides some striking contrasts to its predecessor, the slave narratives: in its use of folklore, *The Conjure Woman* powerfully asserts that blacks do have their own unique traditions and cultural history; in contrast slave narratives, *The Conjure Woman* has but the faintest suggestion that the Christian religion occupies more than a peripheral role in the life of blacks; gone too are stories of "heroic" blacks who made it to freedom. The blacks in *The Conjure Woman* stay home; they are not runaways.

We do find some literary conventions, however. "The characterization of Uncle Julius undeniably borrows heavily from the Harris-Dixon-Page plantation stereotype";[13] and the mythic patterns of conjuring do bear some "resemblance between the Greco-Roman folk tales collected in Ovid's *Metamorphoses*."[14] But one would be mistaken to attribute the imaginative and emotional powers of *The Conjure Woman* solely to folk tale restatement, for as William Andrews reveals, "Only 'The Goophered Grapevine' had specific folklore origins, Chesnutt maintained; the remainder of [*The Conjure Woman*] was 'the fruit of my own [Chesnutt's] imagination....'"[15] In fashioning *The Conjure Woman*, Chesnutt constructed a unique reservoir fed by the ancient currents of protest and over whose banks spilled the rising waters of African American folk lore, pride, and humanism: the clearer waters of black self-definition.

Chesnutt's characters in *The Conjure Woman* are not fully developed. They are sketches, types, caricatures. Given the fablistic nature of the stories though, this is to be expected. More importantly, the characters are not idealized; and except for Julius none of the characters are mulattoes wavering in some racial limbo--each is entirely black. Some are selfish; but some are not. Some are jealous, some are not. Blacks, Chesnutt implies are no different from whites--some are more admirable than others. Perhaps because Uncle Julius' stories are highly moralistic, cleverly psychological, and are meant to illustrate the invisible threads of humanity from which both blacks and whites are woven, some readers have been uncomfortable with Julius' characterization. His stories decry man's inhumanity to man, while Julius himself seems to have forsaken democratic principles in lieu of economic considerations--but this is like blaming Scheherazade for saving her own life by telling her *Arabian Nights* stories.

There remains the question of why Chesnutt, in 1899, chose to tell antebellum slave stories. One reason was to belie the popular plantation tradition which painted a rosy picture of the Old South.[16] Another, more important, reason was that even after three decades, the promise of emancipation had not yet been fulfilled; as a result, blacks still felt it necessary to prove that they too were humans who felt, loved and acted like other humans.

Using Uncle Julius as a mouthpiece, Chesnutt's strategy was to tell seven stories, all of which illustrated the emotional lives of blacks. Many critics have suggested there is no central theme to the tales. I propose to show that the two themes discussed in the earlier slave narratives--the break up of the family and the strong bonds of love that endured even in slavery--bind these tales into a unified vision. Each tale draws upon and is given additional emotional power from these themes.

The first tale in *The Conjure Woman*, "The Goophered Grapevine," has been read as a parable "which explains the consequences of an unbound faith in economic progress and the way such a belief serves to conceal the cost in human dignity."[17] Certainly, it is that. But the story of Henry, the black slave who is "goophered" by eating conjured grapes and whose life's vitality thereafter mirrors the seasonal growth cycle of the grapevines (he is rejuvenated in spring, moribund in winter), echoes the Demeter/Persephone myth, not only in its use of seasonal growth fluctuations, but also in its implied analogy to the slaves' abduction from Mother-Africa. I make this claim despite the fact that Demeter, who "is best known as the sorrowing mother,"[18] has no direct parallel in "The Goophered Grapevine"; no one mourns Henry's death. But, by signifying the Demeter myth, Chesnutt's suggestion is clear: that under the system of slavery, as all men are bound to the soil and the work of the seasons, as all men are subjected to exploitation by their masters, so too all "slave mothers" are "sorrowing mothers." This theme, admittedly, has only faint resonance in this first tale. But as a frame story (as all the tales are) its structure implies a subtextual message. One reading, as already mentioned has political overtones; but the central purpose of the conjure stories is to bring the slave characters "out of the shadows of their anonymity and separate slave status and into the light of a common humanity with the reader,"[19] a careful reading must look beyond a strictly economic reading. Certainly, Chesnutt makes this clear in his depiction of John (the book's white narrator) as a shallow, one-dimensional man preoccupied with economic and materialistic interests, while his wife, Annie, is cast more firmly as the compassionate and spiritually attuned interpreter. It is Annie's keen sense of sympathy which keys the reader's response generally.

There is further evidence as well that the shadow of the "sorrowing mother" hovers over all of the tales. No one can fail to see in "Sis Becky's Pickaninny" the theme of the "sorrowing mother." In that tale, Becky, who has lost her husband, found comfort in the fact she still had her son, Mose. But her master, in order to purchase a race horse, trades Becky for the horse, separating the mother from her son. Mose begins to pine away; Becky feels she is going to die. Only conjuring reunites them.

In "The Gray Wolf's Ha'nt" a conjure man whose son has been killed, seeks revenge on the murderer, Dan. Whether justly or not, the conjure man's grief drives him to trick Dan into killing his own wife, Mahaly. When Dan realizes that he has been tricked, Dan's revenge is to kill the conjure man, but in doing so, Dan is tricked again, and forever assumes the form of a wolf. "The Gray Wolf's Ha'nt," therefore, contains two stories of men driven by grief to revenge the loss of their loved one. One is a "sorrowing" father, the other a "sorrowing" husband.

The theme of "sorrowing" unites "Sis Becky's Pickaninny," "The Gray Wolf's Ha'nt," and "The Goophered Grapevine." Further, the white master McAdoo, whose blind revenge in the Civil War causes his death in "The Goophered Grapevine"--"he des want ter kill a Yankee fer eve'y dollor he los' 'long er dat grape-raisin' Yankee" (p. 32)--signifies that a more complex thematic relationship is being drawn to illustrate the similarity of passion between the black characters in these tales and their white counterparts. Thus two themes bind whites and blacks together and are held up for examination: both races mourn the loss of their loved ones; both are capable of the furious emotion of revenge.

Chesnutt's fashioning of tales that restate and reinforce the significance and universality of these themes is a masterful stroke. That is why Richard Baldwin's claim that "Sis Becky's Pickaninny" is "not an integral part of a larger conception" is myopic.[20] Baldwin's additional claim that "The Gray Wolf's Ha'nt" "has no taint of propaganda" also fails to realize the larger relationship the tales have to one another. That is why criticism concerning "The Gray Wolf's Ha'nt" which claims, as Nancy Ann Gidden has, there is "Nothing [which] accounts for his [Julius's] choice of a plot or the tragic nature of the tale he tells; nothing, that is, except coincidence..." is wrong. Gidden goes on to say that without Annie as a listener and proper interpreter "the sense of unified form characteristic of [the] other conjure tales is missing."[21] The form might be altered, but as this is the sixth tale of seven, the reader no longer requires Annie's sensitivity, no longer must see a direct link drawn between blacks and whites to respond sympathetically to the tragedy of the black characters.

The story "Po' Sandy," like "Sis Becky's Pickaninny," has as its most obvious theme, the blatant disregard slave masters had for their slaves' families. Sandy, who is a hard worker, is moved from household to household so all of the slavemaster's children can enjoy his labors. Ironically, because he is a good worker, and because his slavemaster wants to be fair to his own children, Sandy's family life is destroyed. Upon returning to the plantation for his rotation there, Sandy finds his wife has been sold.

> One time w'en Sandy wuz lent out ez yushal, a spekilater come erlong wid a lot er niggers, en Mars Marrabo swap Sandy's wife off fer a noo 'oman. W'en Sandy come back, Mars Marrabo gin 'im a dollar, en 'lowed he wuz monst'us sorry fer ter break up de fambly, but de spekilater had gin 'im a big boot, en times wuz hard en money skase, en so he wuz bleedst ter make de trade. Sandy tuk on some 'bout losin' his wife, but he soon seed dey want to use cryin' ober spilt merlasses.... (pp. 42-43)

Sandy's next wife, Tenie, is a conjurer, and changes Sandy into a tree so that Sandy "could stay on de plantation for a w'ile" (p. 45). But while Tenie was away one day, Sandy was cut down and taken to the saw mill and cut into boards.

Chesnutt's assault on the insensitivity of slave owners to their slaves' families is obvious here. What is not so apparent as a result of Sandy's transfiguration, is Chesnutt's comment of lynching. Just as in *Clotel*, when Currer is made to witness the burning of a slave who dared to run away and then raise his hand to his master, Chesnutt's Sandy also, through conjuring, tries to escape his bondage and defy his master's will. Eugene Terry's insights about "Po' Sandy" are worth reviewing:

> Removal from reality through metamorphoses cannot hide the reality of a brutal killing. One is reminded, as Chesnutt surely intended, of the factual records of killings of runaway slaves. The reader cannot miss the point that slavery made this dreadful scene necessary. The reader is forced, with Annie, to exclaim, "What a system it was ... under which such things were possible" (p. 60).[22]

In a similar vein, Trudier Harris's chapter "Literary Lynchings and Burnings," opens with a comment on the above mentioned scene from *Clotel*. And though Harris does not focus on "Po' Sandy," her comments about *Clotel* quite naturally reinforce Terry's position: "Brown's novel is the first in a long line of works in which black American writers show black people being summarily executed for some 'offense' against whites."[23] Werner Sollors notwithstanding, this is not the sort of cultural adjustment one finds in Jewish, or any other, American literature. Undoubtedly, this is the most dehumanizing example of black powerlessness in *The Conjure Woman*.

"Mars Jeem's Nightmare" has usually been quickly discussed and dismissed as a turn-about tale, in which a white slave owner, Jim McLean, is turned into a slave for a short time, and as a result, later becomes a kind, more considerate master. What needs to be stressed more often is the reason for McLean's physical and spiritual transformation. And that reason is that McLean had sent away the girl friend of slave Solomon who *wisely* gives McLean a lesson by having him conjured.

This story works on three levels. In Solomon's case, the story exposes the injustice of slavery and its destructive effect upon family and love bonds. For McLean, his change of heart results in his gaining the once-denied love of his sweetheart, Libbie McSwayne. And in the frame's parallel story, Uncle Julius is able to touch Annie's heart, thus getting his lazy grandson, Tom, reinstated on the farm. The sanctity of love bonds are roundly applauded in this tale.

"The Conjurer's Revenge" occupies a fascinating position in black literature. In this tale, the "black as mule" trope plays out literally what other works can only suggest symbolically. Chesnutt is the first to mythologize this folk theme in African American literature, and his tale has its descendants in Hurston's *Their Eyes Were Watching God* and *Mules and Men*, and also in Alice Walker's *The Color Purple*.[24]

Of all the tales, this one's preoccupation with family bonds is the slightest. And when they are portrayed, it is comically. The story deals with the slave Primus who, for stealing a conjurer's shote, is turned into a mule. As a result, everyone assumes Primus is a runaway. While another slave, Dan, is driving Primus-the-mule in the fields, Dan sees Sally, Primus' wife, and shines up to her. About to kiss her, Dan feels a blow to the scruff of his neck, delivered by Primus-the-mule. Later, Primus gets another opportunity to kick Dan so severely that Dan is laid up for a couple of days. While Dan is recovering, the mule taunts Dan through his cabin window and even tries to break down the cabin door.

Often given less serious attention due to its comic nature, "The Conjurer's Revenge" is a powerfully effective tale. By literally making the slave a mule, as the institution of slavery metaphorically does, Chesnutt was able to show that even as a mule, slaves were emotional and had strong love bonds that could not be altered under any conditions. The frame's parallel story is also revealing. In it, Julius convinces John to buy not a mule, but a horse--and, of course, Julius knows someone who has a horse for sale. In three months, the horse is diseased and wind-broken; John realizes he has been conned. If John resents Julius' deceit, he should no less resent McAdoo's deceitful selling of Henry at high prices in the spring and then rebuying him cheaply in the fall in "The Goophered Grapevine." More widely read readers might also recall William Wells Brown's experience while let out to "Dick" Miller--Brown was ordered to blacken the gray hairs of older slaves about to be sold in order to make them appear younger than they were.[25] Not being misled by appearances is an obvious caution; more importantly, the listener is shown that even the institution of slavery could not eradicate a black man's humanity.

The Conjure Woman's final tale is "Hot Foot Hannibal." Its beginning describes the hot-headed Mabel, John's sister-in-law, breaking off her engagement with Malcolm Murchison. Later, while the family is out for a carriage ride, Julius relates a tale when their horse balks at seeing "Chloe's ha'nt." The inner frame tale is about the love of slaves Jeff and Chloe, a love which is jeopardized by their master, Dugal' McAdoo. McAdoo's intervention--he plans to marry Chloe not to Jeff but to Hannibal--results ultimately in another lesson about the deception of appearances, and the tragic death of both Jeff and Chloe. Julius' story of love gone wrong cools off Mabel's hot head and rekindles her love for Murchison. And thus the story, and the book, close on a "happy" note of reconciliation--though it is only for the whites involved.

Chesnutt's *The Conjure Woman* is a fascinating, inventive piece of prose. Its appeal for the humane treatment of blacks was sensitive, balanced, and indirect, though only the most obtuse reader could have failed to see Chesnutt's meaning. Chesnutt's portrayal of conjuring was a cry for black autonomy, for in its use, Chesnutt rejected the assimilationist theories that the American melting pot represented. There would be no official amalgamation of opposites in America if that meant blending Christianity with paganism or white blood with black blood. Chesnutt also recognized that some of his tales had their counterparts in Greco-Roman tradition; but getting whites to recognize and acknowledge those cultural similarities was no easy task. And when it came to miscegenation, white men acted one way in public, another in private. Together, Chesnutt's *The Conjure Woman* and Brown's *Clotel* are part of the black literary tradition whose message begged to be heard: "I am a man."

Mark Twain's *Huckleberry Finn* [26] (1885), although obviously not part of the African American canon, made the same eloquent plea for the dignity and humanity of African Americans and deserves some mention here, too.

Huck's journey down river with Jim allowed Huck--a boy with as ingrained a penchant for deceit, lies, and verbal improvisation as the stereotypic slave--to realize Jim's human qualities, qualities which transform Jim in Huck's eyes from a comic, superstitious, stereotypic slave into a man. Addressing his white audience through the mouthpiece of Huck, Twain reveals Jim's humanity in a manner similar to Chesnutt's and Brown's strategies: in a number of scenes, Twain illustrates the strength of familial bonds in the slave family and, as a result, Huck comes to realize that Jim in no less human than himself. One such scene occurs in Chapter XXIII, after Huck awakes on the raft to find Jim crying:

> When I waked up, just at day-beak, he [Jim] was setting there with his head down betwixt his knees, moaning and mourning to himself. I didn't take notice, nor let on. I knowed what it was about. He was thinking about his wife and his children, away up yonder, and he was low and homesick; because he hadn't ever been away from home before in his life; and I do believe he cared just as much for his people as white folks does for their'n. It don't seem natural, but I reckon it's so. (p. 124)

Later, in Chapter XXVII, after the king has swindled the Wilks family and then sells their slaves to traders, Huck is witness to the three Wilks girls grieving because their family of slaves has been broken up by the traders. The grief of the broken-up slave family is no less stirring.

> ...the king sold them [the traders] the niggers reasonable ... and away they went, the two sons up the river to Memphis, and their mother down the river to Orleans. I thought them poor [Wilks] girls and them niggers would break their hearts for grief; they cried around each other, and took on so it most made me down sick to see it.... I can't ever get it out of my memory, the sight of them poor miserable girls and niggers hanging around each other's necks and crying.... (pp. 144-45)

Huck's decision later in the novel to side with Jim in his renunciation of the Widow Watson's and slavery's claim to Jim was, according to Ralph Ellison, a "pivotal moment" in the development of Huck's character and the novel's plot. Ellison explained why:

> Huck Finn has struggled with the problem poised by the clash between property rights and human rights, between what the community considered to be the proper attitude toward an escaped slave and his knowledge of Jim's humanity, gained through their adventures as fugitives together. He has made his decision on the side of humanity. In this passage [the one in which Huck tears up his letter to the Widow Watson and declares he'll go to hell] Twain has stated the basic moral issue centering around Negroes and the white American's democratic ethics....
> Huck Finn knew, as did Mark Twain, that Jim was not only a slave but a human being, a man who in some ways was to be envied, and who expressed his essential humanity in his desire for freedom, his will to possess his own labor, in his loyalty and capacity for friendship and in his love for his wife and child.[27]

Twain's *Huckleberry Finn*, presented a portrait of a black American in a way which humanized him to white audiences. It represents an important step for American literature generally, not only because in it Hemingway claimed that American literature began, but because Twain, as a white writer, took seriously the humanity of the

African American and brought that humanity to life on the printed page. If Chesnutt was writing to counter the currents of apologist plantation writers, so too was Twain.

I have claimed that the portrayal of the black man's humanity was a theme common to nineteenth century African American literature. In the works of Twain, too, we discover this important theme; that he believed it was important, is evidenced by the fact that he made it the subject of another of his novels, *Pudd'nhead Wilson* (1894). Twain's skill and sensitivity to the issue of a black man's humanity prompted Langston Hughes to write about Twain and his characterization of blacks in *Pudd'nhead Wilson* that:

> Mark Twain, in his presentation of Negroes as human beings, stands head and shoulders above the other Southern writers of his time, even such distinguished ones as Joel Chandler Harris, F. Hopkins Smith, and Thomas Nelson Page. It was a period when most writers who included Negro characters in their work at all, were given to presenting the slave as ignorant and miserable, and all Negroes as either comic servants on the one hand or dangerous brutes on the other. That Mark Twain's characters in *Pudd'nhead Wilson* fall into none of these categories is a tribute to his discernment. And that he makes them neither heroes nor villains is a tribute to his understanding of human character.[28]

Women, too, played a role in the development of their image as good mothers, good wives, and good people. It is to this literary record, and its legacy in modern African American writings that I now turn in the next chapter.

NOTES

1. *The Souls of Black Folk*, in *Three Negro Classics* (New York: Signet, 1968), p. 221.

2. Frederick Douglass, *Narrative of the Life of Frederick Douglass: An American Slave* (New York: Signet, 1968); William Wells Brown, *Clotel; or, The President's Daughter [with a Sketch of the Author's Life]* (New York: Citadel Press, 1969)--the narrative sketch of Brown's life prefaces this edition of *Clotel*. (Brown wrote a full length slave narrative, but the citation herein do not refer to any of those editions.) All references to these texts are from these editions and are marked by page number in parentheses.

Although Brown's *Clotel* has long been honored as the first novel by an African American, Henry Louis Gates, Jr., has suggested that that honor be given to James William's fraudulent slave narrative, which appeared in *Anti-Slavery Examiner*, in serialization, beginning February 15, 1838. Gates argues: "I submit that we reclaim this wonderful lost text from abolitionist authentication, shift it from the bibliographical category of fraudulent or dubious slave narratives, and give it its rightful place as the first *novel* in the African American tradition. For what else can a fictionalized slave narrative be?" See: "From Wheatley to Douglass: The Politics of Displacement," in *Frederick Douglass: New Literary and Historical Essays*, ed. Eric J. Sundquist (Cambridge: Cambridge University Press, 1990), p. 59.

3. *William Wells Brown and Clotelle: A Portrait of the Artist in the First Negro Novel* (Hamben, CT: Archon Books, 1969), pp. 76-90.

4. Richard O. Lewis, "Literary Conventions in the Novels of William Wells Brown," *College Language Association Journal* 29 (December 1985): p. 129.

5. Ibid, p. 131.

6. Ibid, p. 8.

7. Married women were not granted legal joint custody rights

to their children until 1860 in New York State; later elsewhere, except Mississippi. See: Linda K. Kerber and Jane De Hart-Mathews, *Women's America: Refocusing the Past* (New York: Oxford University Press, 1987), pp. 474-75.

8. *Narrative*, p. 23.

9. "The Wife of His Youth" in *"The Wife of His Youth" and Other Stories of the Color Line* (Ann Arbor: University of Michigan Press, 1969); *The Conjure Woman* (Ann Arbor: The University of Michigan Press, 1969). All references to these texts that follow will be marked by page numbers in parentheses.

10. *Beyond Ethnicity: Consent and Descent in American Culture* (New York: Oxford University Press, 1986). All citations refer to this edition and are marked by page numbers in parentheses.

11. Chesnutt chose not to "pass" in his mature years. It could be argued that when his first short stories were published in the *Atlantic Monthly* (beginning with "The Goophered Grapevine" in 1887), Chesnutt was ostensibly passing as white. But, a decade later, the success of Chesnutt's *The Conjure Woman* and *The Wife of His Youth and Other Stories of the Color Line* convinced Houghton Mifflin to become the "first major publishing house in the United States to underwrite an Afro-American novel, a fact which suggests that Chesnutt's racial identity was clearly known by that time. See: William L. Andrews, Foreward to *The House Behind the Cedars* (Athens, GA: University of Georgia Press, 1988), p. ix.

12. In *The Immigrant Experience in America*, ed. Frank J. Coppa and Thomas J Curran (Boston: Twayne Publishers, 1976), p. 184.

13. James R. Giles, "Chesnutt's Primus and Annie: A Contemporary View of *The Conjure Women*," *Markham Review* 3 (February 1972): p. 46.

14. Karen Magee Myers, "Mythic Patterns in Charles Waddell Chesnutt's *The Conjure Woman* and Ovid's *Metamorphoses*," *Black American Literary Forum* 13 (spring 1979): p. 13.

15. *The Literary Career of Charles W. Chesnutt* (Baton Rouge: Louisiana State University Press, 1980), p. 45.

16. Robert Farnsworth speculates that a letter he reprints by Chesnutt's daughter, probably "echoes her father's feeling": "This book of plantation tales as told by 'Uncle Julius' in the dialect of North Carolina Negro was quite different in point of view from the plantation

stories of George W. Cable, Thomas Nelson Page, Harry Stillwell Edwards, and others of that school. There was no glossing over the tragedy of slavery; there was no attempt to make the slave-master relationship anything but what it actually was." Farnsworth himself writes the following about Chesnutt's novel: "The inner stories of Uncle Julius convey the indictment Chesnutt wanted to make of the master-slave relationship in implicit rebuttal of the sentimental picture that had become current in the magazine fiction of the time." See the Introduction to *The Conjure Woman* (Ann Arbor: University of Michigan Press, 1969), pp. vii, xiii.

Also: Robert Hemenway writes that Joel Chandler Harris' Uncle Remus stories were part of the romantic tradition which tried to picture slavery days in a good light: "By referring to the romantic tradition of the plantation, a warm, mythic memory that had existed in the South since the proslavery fiction of John Pendleton Kennedy in the 1830s, Harris reinforced a historical theory of slavery that began with the premise, widespread in his generation, that the human relationships of the peculiar institution had been close and mutually supporting. There is relatively little truth to this assertion, especially from black people's point of view, but it was a premise that could be manipulated to enlist support for the cause of the New South." It is this romantic tradition which *The Conjure Woman* was trying to counter. See: Introduction to *Uncle Remus: His Songs and His Sayings* by Joel Chandler Harris (New York: Penguin Books, 1982), p. 21.

17. Theodore R. Hovet, "Chesnutt's 'The Goophered Grapevine' as Social Criticism," *Black American Literary Forum* 7 (fall 1973): p. 88.

18. Michael Stapleton, *A Dictionary of Greek and Roman Mythology* (New York: Bell Publishing Company, 1978), p. 65.

19. William Andrews, *The Literary Career of Charles W. Chesnutt*, p. 58.

20. "The Art of *The Conjure Woman*," *American Literature* 43, no. 3 (November 1971): p. 391.

21. "'The Gray Wolf's Ha'nt'": Charles W. Chesnutt's Instructive Failure," *College Language Association Journal* 27 (June 1984): pp. 408, 410.

22. "The Shadow of Slavery in Charles Chesnutt's *The Conjure Woman*," *Ethnic Groups* 4 (1982): p. 113.

23. *Exorcising Blackness: Historical and Literary Lynchings and Burning Rituals* (Bloomington: Indiana University Press, 1984), p. 69.

24. The literary trope of "black as mule" is more fully discussed in Chapter IV, which focuses on *The Color Purple*.

25. *Sketch*, p. 21.

26. *Huckleberry Finn* (New York: Norton Critical Edition, 1962), p. 124. All textual citation refer to this edition and are hereafter designated by number in parentheses.

27. *Shadow and Act* (New York: Vintage Books, 1972), p. 31.

28. Introduction to *Pudd'nhead Wilson* by Mark Twain (New York: Bantom Books, 1987), p. xi.

II

THE GOOD MOTHER TRADITION

Harriet A. Jacobs was twenty-seven years old when, in 1845, she escaped from slavery. Some ten years later she began to write what would be one of the very few slave narratives written by a black woman.[1] Published in 1861 under the pseudonym of Linda Brent, Jacobs' narrative, titled *Incidents in the Life of a Slave Girl, Written by Herself*, chronicled her life as a young girl and woman under the peculiar institution, and stressed a number of particular themes meant to pluck the heartstrings and prick the conscience of its intended readership, white northern abolitionists.[2] Jacobs' narrative stressed foremost the integrity and depth of feeling common to all slave families, emphasizing the themes of the slave's sense of duty to family, familial devotion, a mother's love for her children, and a slave mother's dread that her children would be taken from her.

Ten years earlier, Harriet Beecher Stowe's *Uncle Tom's Cabin* had been serialized (1851-1852). Her readers could not have helped but be moved by the Christ-like death of the patient and self-sacrificing slave Uncle Tom, any more than they could have been unmoved by Eliza's heroic escape from slavery by leaping across the treacherous winter ice flows of the Ohio River, babe in arms. But Stowe's fictionalized accounts of slavery (which Stowe claimed were based on factual accounts, and which she documented to defend that claim, in her *A Key to "Uncle Tom's Cabin"*), pale when compared to the factual portrait Jacobs' drew of her own real sacrifices. For seven years she hid in her grandmother's attic crawl space. For seven years she endured a cramped, dark, narrow space, not more than three feet high, without light and ventilation, because from there she could hear her children's voices nearby and draw some solace from their proximity, even though during the ordeal she was unable to reveal herself to them.

When opportunities to escape arose, Jacobs' response was to remain with her children. They, not herself, were first in her thoughts. Jacobs wrote about her children and her bond to them in terms which are, readers of slave narratives recognize, characteristic.

> I could have made my escape alone; but it was more for my helpless children than for myself that I longed for freedom. Though the boon would have been precious to me, above all price, I would not have taken it at the expense of leaving them in slavery. Every trial I endured, every sacrifice I made for their sakes, drew them closer to my heart, and gave me fresh courage to beat back the dark waves that rolled and rolled over me in a seemingly endless night of storms. (pp. 91-92)

Jacobs' narrative was written to appeal to a genteel audience. The voice she assumes in her story is formal, well-educated, and well-read; it also appears to be well versed in the language of sentimental literature, plucking the heartstrings at every offense. Not that such emotional ploys were not deserved; but modern readers may find Jacobs' style overdrawn and blatantly sentimental in its efforts to stir the reader's emotions and indignation.

Jacobs, no doubt to illustrate to her reader that she was educable, eschewed the use of dialect in her narrative, except when recreating the conversations of Southern blacks/slaves. And in the name of decorum, the most ghastly offenses of slavery--the sexual imposition of slave masters upon their female slaves, the brutal beatings, the lynchings--are not related without the appropriate distance and suppression of distasteful detail.[3] Considering Jacobs' audience, her voice and tact was appropriate, though it required that her audience read between the lines. This rhetorical device conveys some of the problems Jacobs faced in telling a white audience the truth about the life of an African American slave girl with absolute candor and accuracy. Regrettably, Jacobs' sense of decorum, her mask, so necessary in her own time, only serves to keep a modern audience at arm's length--the unfortunate result of the author's recognition that discretion was the better part of truth when her audience was white. A reserved narrative results, illustrating the gulf between narrator and audience, as if the fear of being disbelieved or of being calumniated for exaggeration restrains Jacobs' voice.[4]

Decorum and striking the proper narrative tone with her nineteenth century audience did not, however, keep Jacobs from disclosing a number of brutalities to which she was witness during her life as a slave, among them the murder of slaves by their owners, at times for minor offenses (pp. 46,49,52,68,149,155). No reader, past or present, needed to read between the lines when Jacobs claimed, more than once, that death (even if by suicide), was preferable to a life of slavery. For example, upon the death of one of her own infant sons, Jacobs was moved to declare: "Alas, what mockery it is for a slave mother to try to pray back her dying child to life! Death is better than slavery" (p. 63). About another child of hers, she wrote: "When I lay down beside my child, I felt how much easier it would be to see her die than to see her master beat her about, as I daily saw him beat other little ones" (p. 88). On another occasion, Jacobs witnessed a slave's suicide, describing the scene thus:

> Another time I saw a woman rush wildly by, pursued by two men. She was a slave, the wet nurse of her mistress's children. For some trifling offense her mistress ordered her to be stripped and whipped. To escape the degradation and the torture, she rushed to the river, jumped in, and ended her wrongs in death. (p. 124)

For all its deference to the literary tastes of its day, Jacobs' narrative is, nonetheless, a powerful indictment of slavery as well as a remarkable portrait of maternal love and sacrifice in the slave community. Her self-portrait at once transcends stereotype while assuming and reinforcing the venerable status of Black Motherhood.

That Jacobs's narrative should be preoccupied with her role as a mother is, certainly, a result of her gender. Beyond that, Jacobs' decision to remain near her children and to stay in hiding as a strategy to ward off the sexual advances of her master, present a markedly different solution to oppression, than the option of flight taken by males in their narratives.[5] As Houston Baker has commented, an analysis of Jacobs' slave narrative "demonstrates that gender produces striking modifications in the Afro-American discursive subtext. This gender difference does not eradicate the primacy of such governing statements as 'commercial deportation' and 'economics of slavery,' but it does alter and expand their scope."[6]

The expanded discursive subtext that Baker sees in Jacobs' narrative is Jacobs' struggle for sexual autonomy, as is seen in her determination to control her body, particularly, her sexuality and her powers of reproduction, thereby refusing to allow her master to abuse her sexually, either for his own gratification or to create more slaves through the use of her body. Brent had five children with Mr. Sands, a white southerner whom she loved; but she refused to do submit to the lust of her slave master. She does, therefore, come to enunciate a "new code" of behavior, a "new code" of resistance in her slave narrative. Baker has praised Jacobs' narrative, and its subtext, this way: "This new code of ethics emphasized a woman's prerogative to control her own sexuality--to govern the integrity of her body. Articulating such a code in a violently patriarchal system is a monumental and dangerous accomplishment. For 'fatherhood,' under the aspect of southern slavery, assumed all the connotations of 'rape.'"[7] By not attempting a flight to freedom, and by remaining near her family, Jacobs also articulates a value system with values a collective, rather than, individualistic identity. In this collective identity, Baker states, "A new bonding of Afro-American humanity consists, for Brent [Jacobs], in the reunion of mother and child in freedom."[8] These insights are striking for they suggest that despite their common subtexts (the "economics of slavery" and "commercial deportation"), the slave narratives, depending upon the gender of their author, sought aggressively different and contradictory solutions to oppression: flight versus resistance.

Non-fictional portraits of sacrificing mothers, such as Jacobs' narrative, naturally have served as the basis of African American fiction and folklore--this is a function of their palimpsestic nature and their intertextuality. As illustrated in the previous chapter, Charles Chesnutt's "Sis Becky's Pickaninny" is a striking tale of the love bonds between mother and child. In Nella Larson's novel *Passing* (1929), the character Irene Redfield, while arguably an unreliable character, appears nonetheless to be the kind of sacrificing mother who has sublimated her own desires (to the point of vacuity), for the sake of her marriage and her two sons. Likewise, Langston Hughes' character Aunt Hager of *Not Without Laughter* (1930), and Toni Morrison's Eva Peace of *Sula*

(1973), are the kind of mother-figures whose successful characterizations draw much of their strength and solidity from this tradition of self-sacrifice.[9] Based on the intertextuality of this tradition, and its variations (as shall be discussed shortly), this literary and folkloristic tradition might better be characterized as a trope.

Not all portraits of African American mothers are, according to the narrow limits of self-sacrifice and self-denial, positive portrayals, however. There are also portraits of African American mothers who abandon their children. Alice Walker's *Meridian* [10] (1976), is one such novel; in it Walker studies intensively the emotional and spiritual dislocation a young black woman suffers when she disregards the strong communal expectations of her that she be a good mother (and wife) first, and think of herself last. This chapter will focus on *Meridian* shortly.

It is clear that the trope of the good-mother has been strong in African American literature, beginning in the slave narrative and then in works of fiction. In that light, I want to briefly discuss Ann Petry's novel *The Street* [11] (1946), to illustrate that thirty years before the appearance of Alice Walker's *Meridian*, Petry had penned a story so bleakly naturalistic that it forced her main character, Lutie Johnson, into a situation in which abandonment of her only son appeared to be a suitable choice. Petry's novel does not deal with the problems of maternal abandonment, nor the psychological anguish and guilt felt because of such an act, with the intensity that Walker's novel does. In fact, thematically, it is barely an issue in the novel, except indirectly. By which, I mean that Lutie's commitment to keep her son and herself together is so central to her struggle for economic and personal well-being, that the alternative of abandonment never surfaces as an option-- until the novel's close. After Lutie had struggled to keep her son out of harm's way, her decision to abandon him comes, therefore, as a shock. My interest with *The Street* is to show that despite the differences in the novels' treatment of this subject, the option of abandonment for a mother had been dramatized prior to Walker's novel.

The Street deals with life in Harlem, particularly one representative street, 116th Street. In Petry's realization, the street is characterized as a monstrous, devouring creature, a predator crouched to take its prey with shocking, amoral indifference. In its description of the street, the novel comes full circle, beginning and ending with images of garbage and bones set adrift in high winds. Like Steinbeck's use of the turtle as metaphor for the Okies in *The Grapes of Wrath*, Petry's images here serve as metaphor for life in Harlem's streets.

Lutie Johnson, the novel's central character, is an idealistic and hopeful young woman trying to raise her eight-year-old son, Bub. She believes in the American Dream, and has fully embraced the economic ideology of Ben Franklin, believing that hard work will result in personal and financial betterment. At a subtextual level, we recognize that Lutie sees the need to negotiate the economics, not of slavery, but of racism, if she is to be successful and have her piece of the American pie. And certainly, Petry's "street" is a racist and materialistic world. White racism has forced Lutie's husband out of work and into a state of desperation; he turned to drinking and womanizing as a way of proving his manhood. That same racist system has forced Lutie to take work as a house servant, a menial job she wants to leave but finds she can't. It is ironic that much of what Lutie perceives as material accomplishment is the result of her employment as a maid in the white Chandler household. There she is wooed by their opulence (in a way that foreshadows Pauline in *The Bluest Eye*), but neither seduced, nor corrupted. Lutie is a perceptive woman and recognizes that political corruption is part of the reality that secures the Chandler's family wealth. As a servant, she discovers that she is judged with suspicion, and stereotyped as a typical young black woman: lascivious, stealing, and conniving. It is under these circumstances that she comes to live on "the street."

Lutie's one hope out of this trap is her singing voice. But even there, she finds that the talent managers and club owners, who are white, will invest their time on her only if she is willing to grant them sexual favors. In the character "Junto," white racism is personified: his power and money run the clubs, the brothels, and manipulate the talented black jazz artist, Boots Smith. In Junto and the Chandlers, the Franklin ideal is perverted grotesquely, making monetary success not a vehicle for betterment, but for abuse and corruption; it creates a Darwinian world of victims subject to the predations of the powerful.

Upon meeting Lutie, Junto's sexual desire for her exerts an influence on every aspect of her life, exerting control clandestinely over both hers and her son's lives. Junto's sexual craving for Lutie also forces Boots to compromise his integrity (again) and to play a central role in Junto's attempted seduction of Lutie. In these power relationships, there is a clear palimpsestic rewriting of the slave narratives with their indictment of the political rights of slave owners to the bodies of his slaves.

Junto is not the only predator in the novel. *The Street* is littered with them. Each of them is a grotesque; each is indifferent, amoral, resigned, and eager to use other people for his/her own good. The viciousness of these characters and "the street," is brilliantly illustrated by Petry's condensation of time in the novel. Much of the novel is compressed into only two days; the later section of the novel is likewise compressed. Thus, in only a few short days, Lutie and Bub move into an apartment on the street and the integrity of their lives becomes threatened by, among other things, Junto's sexual appetite. Additionally, because Lutie has also put off the sexual advances of her building's superintendent, Jones, he retaliates by involving Bub in mail stealing, a crime for which Bub is caught and jailed.

Thus, despite Lutie's hopes that she and Bub can resist the corrupting influence of the street and exert their own brand of self-determination, they are foiled. Lutie's greatest chance for success is her singing voice, but even this hope is thwarted because she will not compromise her sexual integrity, leaving the impression that, in Petry's naturalistic vision, even the romantic hope that art and jazz can save African Americans and bring them the American Dream is false. For Lutie, her blues and jazz talents do not help her succeed, proving themselves to be an unrealistic hope for a woman not willing to compromise sexually.

In the novel's conclusion, Lutie's frustration with the sexual advances of Junto and Boots, and of Bub's arrest, create such horrific anger in her that, after she thwarts Junto's sexual advances in a staged meeting, she bludgeons Boots to death, and is forced to decide her future in a moment's time. Her decision is to flee New York City for Chicago, and without a word of farewell, she takes flight and abandons Bub to the jail system.

What is so powerfully stunning about Ann Petry's *The Street*, is its unwillingness to romanticize anything, neither its good mother Lutie, nor the blues.[12] What is also so arresting is the quickness and, somehow, the stunning appropriateness of Lutie's flight to save herself.

Lutie has been portrayed throughout the novel as perceptive, leading the reader to conclude that her impressions that she will be better off in Chicago and that Bub may be better off in the social system than with her are not without merit. Nonetheless, Lutie's abandonment is shocking and disturbing. Her devotion to Bub has been unquestionable, and yet she leaves.

Petry's novel is a bleak portrait of city life. And Lutie Johnson's abandonment at once rewrites the good-mother tradition, and expands the trope to include the option of flight. Petry's novel sets the stage for later exploration of the topic of the abandonment of children by their mothers. Alice Walker's *Meridian* would further that exploration. So it is to that novel that this study now turns. But first, a mention of the role of folklore in the construction of identity is essential.

There seems to be little doubt that people tell and listen to folk tales for two reasons. The first is to be entertained. The second is to learn. Often the instructional, or didactic, function of a tale is passive. Cultural anthropologists frequently stress the social function which folklore performs in a culture. Richard Dorson explains that according to William Bascom, folklore has a number of functions:

> Proverbs can settle legal decisions, riddles sharpen wits, myths validate conduct, satirical songs release pent-up hostilities. So the anthropologist searches for context as well as text. A tale is not a dictated text with interlinear translations, but a living recitation delivered to a responsive audience for such cultural purposes as reinforcement of custom and taboo, release of aggressions through fantasy, pedagogical explanations of the natural world, and application of pressures for conventional behavior.[13]

Bruno Bettelheim in his introduction to *The Uses of Enchantment* carefully enumerates the benefits of telling fairy tales to children: they transmit cultural heritage; they convey "the advantages of moral behavior"; they provide a sense of self-worth and a sense of moral obligation; they illustrate that life is difficult, but that its obstacles can be overcome; and they show that "good and evil are omnipresent in life" and part of every man.[14] Fairy tales are a special form of folk tale, admittedly; still everything Bettelheim claims about their function has relevance to other types of folk tales. They are strong purveyors of cultural information, codes of behavior, and they provide a basis for making moral judgments.

Robert Hemenway in his introduction to *Uncle Remus* emphasized the didactic function trickster tales served for black slaves. He wrote:

> The point cannot be overemphasized: black people identified with Brer Rabbit. When Brer Rabbit triumphed over a physically superior foe, black people fantasized themselves in the identical situation. As one black storyteller told an early folklorist: "I allers use my sense for help me 'long jes' like Brer Rabbit." Historian Lawrence Levine states: "The white master could believe that the rabbit stories his slaves told were mere figments of the childish imagination.... Blacks knew better. The trickster's exploits, which overturned the neat hierarchy of the world in which he was forced to live, became their exploits; the justice he achieved, their justice; the strategies he employed, their strategies. From his adventures they obtained relief; for his triumphs they learned hope." Even Harris himself understood this side of Brer Rabbit. In *Nights with Uncle Remus*, Uncle Remus tells the boy, "Well, I tell you dis, ef deze yer tales wuz des fun, fun, fun, en giggle, giggle, giggle, I let you know I'd a-done drapt um long ago."[15]

When Alice Walker copied a Brer Rabbit trickster strategy--of getting what you want by claiming you want its opposite--as a means of getting Sofia released from prison in *The Color Purple*, it is quite clear that for Walker, folklore still can teach, inform, and function.

The premise of this study's use of folklore is that folklore is functional. It is not a ruin; to the contrary, I will argue later, the loss of a culture's folklore can destroy a community. The vitality of folklore should not, however, blind us to the fact that in American society (here I give credit to Sollors' *Beyond Ethnicity*), sometimes the "old ways" are in conflict with America's more progressive "new ways." If we are progressive and desire change, then the old models of behavior espoused by folklore can fail us. Jay Mechling began a recent essay with this statement: "We are so accustomed to talking and writing about folklore as a human strength, as a personal and community resource for enduring, connecting, and celebrating, that we sometimes overlook those instances when folklore fails."[16] The functions of folklore are diverse; and despite its dynamic nature, and the necessary requirement that it be relevant to survive, it can be reactionary. With this in mind, I turn to Alice Walker's *Meridian*. In Meridian Hill's renunciation of her community's customs, she is forced to do what the hero must: redefine her role in society.

Ralph Ellison has called the search for identity "*the* American theme."[17] Frequently that search takes the form of a journey, a loss of innocence, and/or an initiation. Here, we think of Hawthorne's "Young Goodman Brown," Melville's *Moby Dick* (1851), James's *The Portrait of a Lady* (1881), Twain's *Huck Finn* (1885), and Hemingway's *The Sun Also Rises* (1926). We might think also of more recent novels such as *The Catcher in the Rye* (1951), *Invisible Man* (1952), and *To Kill A Mockingbird* (1960); for not surprisingly, as Ellison suggested, "the search for identity" is not a new American theme, but its central enduring preoccupation.

What has changed, however, is the struggle heroes undergo to achieve their new American identity. Goodman Brown grew old as a dour, pessimistic recluse; Ahab's adversary was God and the elements; Huck Finn set off at novel's end for the West; Isabel Archer turned her back on America in favor of Europe; and Jake Barnes suffered emasculation on foreign soil. What the modern era has done is to offer heroes who are made greater for their suffering, not emasculated; they are iconoclasts who are dissatisfied not with mankind but with the traditions and orthodoxies that restrict and restrain men, and so set out to reorder their world, to see it with new eyes, thereby destroying the bastions of tradition, folklore, and sexual stereotypes. It might be said that when those heroes recognize an enemy or adversary, they do not have to search on foreign soil--the enemy they see is here. And yet, those heroes are often hopeful of positive change through the small, though not insignificant, alteration of people as individuals. More than ever before, modern literature questions the wisdom of institutions and elevates the value of the individual. This is not to say that all traditions are thrown out; but each appears to be given a more serious analysis to ensure its continued worth within a quickly changing society.

The usefulness and the limitations of traditions and folklore have been presented as a central theme in the novels *Invisible Man* and *To Kill A Mockingbird*. These issues also preoccupy a great deal of Alice Walker's attention. And it is with these double-edged swords--tradition and folklore--that Walker tests and probes the fabric of American society, and, primarily, the blacks who live within it. For Walker's central character in *Meridian*, Meridian Hill, the search for identity involves the slow and painful transcendence of both the folklore of Black Motherhood, and the stereotypes of racism.

The central characters in Alice Walker's *Meridian* and in her later novel *The Color Purple* are women who struggle successfully to break free of the stifling traditions, lore, and stereotypes of black womanhood. Interestingly, the primary focus of Meridian Hill's story, set in the political ferment of the 1960s, concerns itself with issues of an intellectual and spiritual nature; in contrast, Celie's story (*The Color Purple*), is told in a context which for the most part is removed from "racial issues" and focuses on her struggle to subvert the physical and economic bondage that rules her early life. For Walker, the novels represent part of what has become the central preoccupation of her work: exploring the nature of "black womanhood and its myriad shadings."[18]

Walker's attempts to redefine the role of black women within the community of blacks and the larger framework of American society, presents her character Meridian with a dilemma that shakes her to her foundation: As a political activist, should she kill others, or should she reject that radical option for change? In the context of the political setting of the novel, the question of killing in the name of social revolution, appears, despite its relevance, somewhat distant and academic. But on a personal level, Meridian is all too often forced to decide which of her culture's traditional teachings and modes of behavior are worth preserving and which must be overturned.

Using a technique that recalls *To Kill A Mockingbird*, *Invisible Man*, and *The Catcher in the Rye*, the novel's main body is retrospective; *Meridian* begins with its central character at the zenith of her powers, in a state of "enlightenment." Walker establishes this notion by prefacing the novel with a definition of the word "meridian." The word's twelve connotations include: "the highest point reached by a heavenly body in its course"; "the highest point of power, prosperity, splendor, etc; zenith; apex; culmination;" and "southern [rare]." The novel then begins with Truman Held arriving by car in the southern town of Chicokema, Georgia, at the same time that Meridian is defying the town's racist policies by staring down an old military tank painted, significantly, white. The reason for the confrontation is that the town's black children want to view the body of "Marilene O'Shay, One of the Twelve Wonders of the World" (p. 19). A sign decries that O'Shay was once an "Obedient Daughter," a "Devoted Wife," an "Adoring Mother," as well as a woman "Gone Wrong" (p. 19). Further, the woman is described as once having been "an ideal woman, a 'goddess'" (p. 20). Observing Meridian's defiance of the police, Truman remarks to a townsman about the O'Shay sideshow: "That's got to be a rip-off" (p. 19). What Truman recognizes with such apparent ease, Meridian has learned through the experience of her life: that the stereotypic language used to delimit the roles of women are stifling and anachronistic. In the novel's opening scene, Walker deftly presents one of the central themes of the novel: that the two major obstacles to black women in American society are racism and sexism. It is a theme more explicitly stated later in the novel during Meridian's years at Saxon College: "Meridian and the other students felt they had two enemies: Saxon, which wanted them to become something--ladies--that was already obsolete, and the larger, more deadly enemy, white racist society" (p. 95).

Meridian's growth as a character depends upon her increasing awareness of the dangers inherent in the traditional mores of African American life. As a girl, her most pressing problem is dealing with her mother. This is a formidable task, for Meridian views her mother in a context which is larger than just the relationship between the two of them: "Meridian thought of her [mother] as Black Motherhood personified, and of that institution she was in terrible awe, comprehending as she did the horror, the narrowing of child, it had invariably meant" (pp. 96-97). Even more intimidating, Meridian also believed "her mother was a giant" (p. 122).

Because Mrs. Hill is a giant, Meridian faces the task of metaphorically slaying her--even if the symbolic slaying spawns grief and guilt. According to the critic Peter Erickson:

> Meridian's troubled feelings about her mother revolve around
> the conflict between the need to love her mother--"it is death
> not to love one's mother"--and the need to be different from

her. Meridian is unable to break away easily from her mother because "an almost primeval guilt" prevents her from criticizing her mother.[19]

The feminist critic Karen Rowe refers to similar difficulties confronting contemporary women. In her discussion of fairy tales and other "romantic" literature, Rowe postulates that within a patriarchal society women are doomed to feelings of guilt and regret whether they remain within or outside of their traditionally prescribed roles:

> Fairy tales, therefore, do acknowledge traumatic ambivalences during a female's rite of passage; they respond to the need for both detachment from childish symbioses and a subsequent embracing of adult independence. Yet, this evolution dooms female protagonists (and readers) to pursue adult potentials in one way only: the heroine dreamily anticipates conformity to those predestined roles of wife and mother. As Adrienne Rich so persuasively theorizes in *Of Woman Born*, the unheralded tragedy with western patriarchies is found in this mother/daughter relationship. If she imitates domestic martyrdom [as Mrs. Hill does], the daughter may experience a hostile dependency, forever blaming the mother for trapping her within a constricting role. If a daughter rebels [as Meridian does], then she risks social denunciation of her femininity, nagging internal doubts about her gender identity, and rejection by a mother who covertly envying her daughter's courage must yet overtly defend her own choices. Furthermore, romantic tales point to a complicity of women within a patriarchal culture, since as primary transmitters and models for female attitudes, mothers enforce their daughters' conformity.[20]

How Meridian is able to transcend the limits of "Black Motherhood" and the grief and guilt that burden her as a result are presented by Walker in a meandering series of episodes which,

> continually [drop] the scene and later [return] to it for a fresh look; intricacy and intensity are built up by this circling back to take up another facet of the mother-daughter relationship, to press the analysis further. Walker establishes a frame of

reference in the present from which she can delve into the past. Meridian's mother is introduced in a flashback within a flashback as 'the past' which cannot be ignored.[21]

But because Mrs. Hill represents, even in Meridian's mind, something greater than herself, the narrative effect of looking backward suggests that Walker, through the eyes of her cynosure, is also passing judgment on the terribly inadequate and debilitating folklore of Black Motherhood.

Meridian's first split from her mother comes while attending church at the age of thirteen, the onset of her womanhood. There, Meridian is swept-up by the effects of the music the congregation sings, though it is her father's voice she singles out. In that voice, Meridian recognizes for the first time, an anguish that seemed to be "resigned to death" (p. 29). Mrs. Hill prompts her daughter then to accept Christ, but Meridian cannot; for she senses in the music a resignation to suffering, to a tradition of slavery and oppression which promises no chance for change on earth. Meridian's recognition and refusal to accept the traditional church of her parents results in the loss of her mother's love (p. 28).

Part of the reason Meridian rejects her mother's brand of religion is that she senses her mother lacks the kind of earthly spirituality her father recognizes in the American Indian; another reason is that Mrs. Hill attended a church whose message, half the time, was "incomprehensible" (p. 78). Not surprisingly, therefore, when the time comes to tutor Meridian about the dangers of sex, Mrs. Hill relied upon language that Meridian found more figurative than effective: "...her mother only cautioned her to 'be sweet.' She [Meridian] did not realize this was a euphemism for 'keep your panties up and your dress down,' an expression she had heard and been puzzled by" (p. 60). As a result, Meridian's pregnancy "came as a total shock" (p. 61).

Mrs. Hill, and women like Eddie's mother, Meridian's mother-in-law, are doubly at fault for their failure to properly school Meridian in the dangers of sex. Then, after Meridian is pregnant, instead of giving her useful advice, they promulgate old wives' tales: "It is not possible to become pregnant if love is made standing up" (p. 63); and, that intercourse during pregnancy could weaken the baby's brain (p. 65). A negligence even more pernicious was that Mrs. Hill never cautioned Meridian unambiguously against either sex or marriage. This duplicitous "oversight" is not only ironic, in light of Mrs. Hill's regrets about having to sacrifice her teaching career, her tranquility, and her identity to a man and a family (p. 50), but also tragic in light of the effects on Meridian's life. The result is that, just as Mrs. Hill's submission to the role of Black Motherhood caused her to become "distracted from who she was" (p. 50), Meridian's unwitting role in her mother's loss of identity, and then her own remorse about giving up her own child, create within Meridian two sources of guilt from which she must extirpate herself.

Meridian's dilemma is staggering for, at a very young age, she has already, like the stereotypic descriptions of the mummy (a pun on mommy) of Mrs. O'Shay, been characterized by a long list of attributes that restrict her: "She was only seventeen. A drop-out from high school, a deserted wife, a mother, a daughter-in-law" (pp. 75-76). The role of motherhood especially is a difficult one for Meridian. She likens her new-born son's demands on her to slavery: "he [Eddie, Jr.] did not feel like anything to her but a ball and chain" (p. 69); she dreams "of ways to murder him." In the matter of her husband's eventual infidelity and desertion, there is not a hint of indignation or remorse from either her mother or mother-in-law, both of whose responses are conditioned by the folk wisdom of African American women:

> But he was "good" to her, even then. He did not "cheat" and "beat" her both, which meant he was "good" to her, according to her mother, his mother, the other women in the neighborhood and in fact just about everyone she knew, who seemed to expect the two occurrences together, like the twin faces of a single plague. (p. 65)

The greatest psychological hurdle for Meridian to overcome is her desertion of her son, an act which is a direct affront to the history of Black Motherhood and, most particularly, Meridian's own valorous and indomitable ancestors. Among those courageous women ancestors was a slave who stole back her sold children, was whipped nearly to death as punishment, and yet kept her family together by subsisting on the meager fruits of the woods and streams. There was also a slave who "bought not only her own freedom, but that of her husband and children as well" (p. 123). Meridian's grandmother endured beatings and a philandering husband (i.e., a "bad" husband). And Mrs. Hill, though she had to suffer a father who was against her being educated, had been blessed with a selfless mother who endured twelve pregnancies and worked outside the home to provide for Mrs. Hill's education. It was against this legacy of sacrifice and suffering that Meridian found herself rebelling.

If Walker's women in *Meridian* have unwittingly been duped into believing that their purpose in life is defined by their family's needs, and out of complicity continue to perpetuate that role, as the feminists Rowe and Rich suggest, then the ongoing transmission of that role is a type of self-inflicted sexism. But that is not the only brand of sexism Meridian faces. Ironically, the most disillusioning form confronts Meridian at that bastion of "Ladyhood," Saxon College.

It is at Saxon that Meridian encounters sexism at all levels of the institution, from Truman Held, a fellow black student, to the College President. All three of the elder African American males on campus are hypocrites, and two prey upon Meridian's vulnerability by asking sexual favors. This is particularly unnerving for a woman who is torn already by the guilt that accompanies her to college, and by the need to atone for her many "sins." This urge to atone focuses Meridian's attention on the Wild Child;[22] but the Wild Child's death and the resultant confrontation the mourners have with the college's president illustrate a number of salient points. First, Meridian becomes aware that the dignity of one black "child" is of no significance to the larger institution which the college represents. Further, due to the nature of the Wild Child's background, the college's blind eye to her plight is, like Mrs. Hill's ambiguous counsel, a conscious refusal to deal with the larger social issues of African American female sexuality and pregnancy--(after all, Saxon women were by definition, "virgins"). The President of Saxon, like Ellison's Bledsoe, has "greater issues" on his mind:

> [Meridian] imagined the president--a tan, impeccably tailored patriarch with glinting, shifty gray eyes--coming up to The Wild Child's casket and saying, as if addressing a congregation: "We are sorry, young woman, but it is against the rules and regulations of this institution to allow you to conduct your funeral inside this chapel, which, as you may know, was donated to us by one of the finest robber baron families of New York. Besides, it is nearly time for Vespers, and you should have arranged for this affair *through the proper channels* much earlier." (p. 46)

It is the campus guards who serve as the president's authority--the guards who, like the white tank in the novel's opening scene, represent not only "American tradition," [23] but also a particularly malicious brand of sexism prevalent on the campus.

On the campus where "the chimes from the campus clock rang out their inappropriate eighteenth-century melodies" (p. 110), Meridian discovers that in the employ of Professor Raymonds, she must play mouse to his cat in order to get "the extras"--Coke, cookies, tins of tuna, a tennis racket--that she needs to survive on her insufficient scholarship. Hypocritically, Raymonds "was also very emotional about protecting the virtue of black women from white men" (p. 111)--as if he wanted to keep all the despoiling for himself.

It is in Meridian's sexual relationship with Raymonds and with Truman Held, two well-educated black males, that the novel draws an intriguing, albeit dismally pessimistic, portrait of African American males. In the novel's characterizations, both of these men express their sexual appetites and make sexual propositions which, ironically, recall Meridian's first sexual experiences with the mulatto mortician George Daxter, and his assistant. Daxter "tried to pull her on his lap" (p. 66); Raymonds "wanted her to sit on his lap" (p. 112). Daxter's assistant whispers into Meridian's ear, "Think of how it would feel" (p. 66); Truman, while on the way to a party, says to Meridian, "I wish I could make you feel how beautiful it would be with me" (p. 104). That same evening Truman disappears from the party with Lynne Rabinowitz, a white New Yorker and civil rights activist, revealing the depth of his commitment to Meridian.

If the intentions of black males are generally lascivious, and just as often motivated by the color of a woman's skin,[24] then a black woman has little chance of finding and nurturing a mutually beneficial relationship. Realizing this, Meridian aborts the pregnancy which results from her first union with Truman (his ignorance and irresponsibility echoing the president's lack of concern over the fate of the Wild Child). Even during the abortion procedure, Meridian is sexually propositioned by the doctor. "'I could tie your tubes,' he chopped out angrily, 'if you'll let me in on some of all this extra curricular activity'" (p. 115). Later, when Truman returns to Meridian (after his initial tryst with Lynne has ended), he asks her to "Have my beautiful black babies" (p. 116). Meridian's response is to hit Truman with her "green book bag.... Blood dripped onto his shirt" (p. 116). The fury of Meridian's response is fueled by Truman's insensitivity and by Meridian's own furor with her own body:

> It enraged her that she could be made to endure such pain [an abortion], and that he [Truman] was oblivious to it. She was also disgusted with the fecundity of her body that got pregnant on less screwing than anybody's she had ever heard of. It seemed doubly unfair that after all her sexual "experience" and after one baby and one abortion she had not once been completely fulfilled by sex. (pp. 114-15)

That Meridian should not once have felt fulfilled by sex underscores the displacement she feels as a woman whose body is perceived as being the primary measure of her worth.

As a result of the combined failures of her sexual experiences--her refusal to be an "Obedient Daughter," a "Devoted Wife," an "Adoring Mother,"--and her awareness that her education at Saxon College was socially inadequate and hypocritical, Meridian undergoes a spiritual regeneration. She begins by dreaming of death, by having "blue spells," by losing her sight temporarily and by experiencing paralysis; but finally, "she began to experience ecstasy" (p. 119). Meridian's transformation is such that even her roommate Anne-Marion could see all around Meridian's head "a full soft light, as if her head, the spikes of her natural, had learned to glow" (p. 120). Finally, Miss Winters, a black music teacher from Meridian's home town, whispers in Meridian's ear during one of her nightmares about her mother: "I forgive you" (p. 125). Granting Meridian the forgiveness she needed to overcome the "sickness" caused by her rejection of Black Motherhood, Miss Winters, as Mrs. Hill's surrogate, allows Meridian to finally emerge a renewed and revitalized woman.

With the issue of sex, motherhood, and sexism worked-through for Meridian, the issue of racism comes to the foreground, becoming the central focus of the second part of the novel. Walker opts to examine this issue not in epic proportions, but as embodied in the relationship between the white Lynne Rabinowitz and the black Truman Held.

One measure of racism is that the taboos and lore against interracial marriage are almost as numerous (at least in this novel) as those which define the traditional roles of Black Motherhood. There is the story of the rejected and outcast Daxter (p. 65); there is Prof. Raymonds' admonition to Meridian not to mingle with the white South African divinity student (pp. 111-12); there is Lynne's loss of family due to her marriage with Truman (pp. 154-55); there is the death of Camara, Lynne and Truman's daughter; and there is a lode of folklore dealing with the essential empty-headed vacuity of white women, and the perverse drive of white, "lusty young sons" to have sex with any black woman they can (pp. 107-08). And yet, despite all of these taboos, two central characters, Lynne and Truman, marry inter-racially.

The decision to ignore such a vigorous convention is not without its price. Thus, after the novel's first section, in which the characters Meridian and Lynne are characterized as antagonistic opposites, in the second section, Lynne's suffering and character mirrors Meridian's in many significant ways.[25] In fact, because of their common bonds, the two begin to emerge as alter-egos whose coupled religious and racial differences (Christian and Jewish, black and white) allow Walker to create a single "mythic woman," composed of diverse experiences, able to cut across a number of normally insurmountable boundaries. Thus, in Lynne, Walker develops a white female who marries as a college-educated "virgin," has a child who is later murdered, and loves a black man; in Meridian, Walker develops a black female who marries as a young girl, is a high-school drop-out, divorces, abandons her child, and "lets go of men." Together, these women suggest a single "greater consciousness" which allows Walker and the reader to explore two alternate avenues of a perplexing racial issue, manageably reduced in *Meridian* to the question of intra-racial and inter-racial relationships. Walker has attempted in *Meridian* (as she will later in *The Color Purple*), to suggest an androgynous melding of sexual roles as a means of transcending rigid sexual stereotypes;[26] in the character Meridian Hill, Walker creates, through the fusion of a black and a white character, a "colorless mythic woman," who is able to more completely attempt to overcome the color barriers of racism.

In the novel's third section, the fused characters of Meridian and Lynne split and go their separate ways: Lynne appears tragically alienated and alone, her marriage with Truman a failure, her life in ruins, her daughter Camara dead. Meridian is also alone, but she is now motivated by a newborn commitment to the people of her own race.

Meridian's return to her own people is, of course, an expression of her personal and political commitment to the eradication of the twin evils of racism and sexism. But it is only when Meridian chances upon a militant church service that her commitment (and that of the slain Martin Luther King and other activists) appears to be bearing the fruit of a new dream. In the chapter entitled "CAMARA," Meridian attends a service in a church "settled firmly upon the ground." The congregation is singing a song to a familiar melody but the "words sounded quite new to her." Another song, new to her, had words that "were completely hidden from her by the quite martial melody" (p. 195). Gone are the songs of anguish Meridian's father sang. The minister imitated Martin Luther King with effect. He spoke of David and Goliath, and called President Nixon "Tricky Dick." And he "looked down on the young men in the audience and forbade them to participate in the Viet Nam War. He told the young women to stop looking for husbands and try to get something useful in their heads" (p. 195).

The minister urged the slaying of giants (Mrs. Hill "was a giant"); and he urged the young men to be militant and the young women to get an education instead of having babies. The audience's "ah-mens" were spoken in a tone that said "We are fed up." And when an old man stood up to publicly mourn the political murder of his son saying only, "My son died," the tragic deaths of Camara and The Wild Child are likewise recalled--but with an emotional pitch which testifies to a renewed commitment that such killings will no longer be tolerated. Lastly, the church's stained-glass window has supplanted the traditional image of Christ with that of B.B. King with a guitar and a sword (the blues are king, now).

The few remaining chapters follow Meridian's attempts to register black voters. She talks to a black man out of work because he refused to keep the windows where he worked covered up, a sixty-nine year old woman who thinks she's pregnant, and a young girl who was serving time for killing her baby. Respectively, these few people embody, the continued reluctance to become political (like Mrs. Hill, p. 78); the ignorance about womanhood and pregnancy that pervades the poor and remains a legacy for African American women (like the community of Meridian's youth); and the continued anger and fear that grip the young who are not ready to bear children (like the young Meridian). The problems of Meridian's youth still persist, but with a changing church and a personal commitment, the novel suggests that substantive change can happen. But Walker is not a utopian, nor is her character Meridian's idealism unrestrained by the wisdom of personal sorrow. As Meridian leaves the novel, the hat that has become her trademark is left behind for Truman. Truman dons the cap and wonders "...if Meridian knew that the sentence of bearing the conflict in her own soul which she had imposed on herself--and lived through--must now be borne in terror by all the rest of them" (p. 220).

Truman's final thoughts close the novel, and leave the reader wondering: Is the novel ultimately hopeful? I believe it is. But it suggests that change will only come slowly and painfully, and ultimately, only through individual effort and courage. William Mueller had this to say about Ellison's protagonist in *Invisible Man*. It could apply to *Meridian* equally well:

> He has, however, come to certain truths of his own: that conformity to rigid, demeaning conventions and traditions is not the way to health and vitality; that insistence upon such conformity is the weapon of the death-bearing tyrant too power-crazed and fearful to let lives be lived rather than controlled; that "humanity is won by continuing to play in face of certain defeat"; that, despite all the nightmare past, he still loves, and that those who love cannot sustain a permanent underground station.[27]

Meridian Hill is also a person who believes in the humanity of mankind. Her struggle to transcend the conventions and traditions of her culture recalls the theme that Ellison called "the American theme"--the search for identity. Meridian Hill can take her place along side her predecessors: Jake Barnes, the "Invisible Man," Holden Caulfield, Atticus Finch, and a long line of other American heroes, whose quest for identity simultaneously rendered a moral statement about the nature of society.

Meridian Hill can also take her place along side a tradition of African American literary characters, some real, some fictional, who have striven to enlarge the status of women and the integrity of women's place in African American society. Along with Harriet Jacobs and Lutie Johnson, Alice Walker's character, Meridian Hill has helped redefine the options of resistance for African American women, in the face of racism, and in the face of sexism.

These three works continue to illustrate the need for African Americans to negotiate the economics of slavery/racism in America. They also express an evolution within the literature written by African

American women which begins to embrace individualism, which sees flight and abandonment as options for African American women who feel trapped by circumstances beyond their control. At the same time, this literature, especially as it portrayed in *Meridian*, attempts to expand the definition of family, thereby including the larger African American community and its broader political concerns. Seen in these terms, Meridian's life trials mirror the hero cycle as described by Joseph Campbell: flight, the call to adventure, the slaying of "giants," the discovery of a helper, the test, the triumph, and the return to society with a boon.[28] Maybe it is not possible to write and read stories about women who abandon their families and then seek to redefine themselves, and therefore their society, without recalling the mythic patterns of the Hero Cycle and the Call to Adventure. And because both the Western tradition and African American slave narratives most often have males fulfilling the role of adventurer (the hero who leaves his family behind), the placement of women in those literary roles will invite comparison and criticism, a subject which is beyond the scope of this work, but worthy of mention.

Along the way, Jacobs, Petry, and Walker, have enlarged the language, the history, the folk and vernacular conceptions of the trope of Black Motherhood.

NOTES

1. Walter Teller, Introduction to *Incidents in the Life of a Slave Girl* by Linda Brent [Harriet Jacobs] (New York: Harcourt Brace Jovanovich, Publishers, 1973), pp. ix-x.

2. (New York: Harcourt Brace Jovanovich, Publisher, 1973). All references to Jacobs' text refer to this edition and are designated by number in parentheses.

3. Not all sexual detail is omitted, however, since the sexual imposition of slavemaster upon slave was a topic certain to raise the interest and indignation of northern women. See Wilson J. Moses' comments concerning the contrasting treatment of sex as a slave narrative theme in male and female writers, particularly, Douglass' and Jacobs' narratives in "Writing Freely?: Frederick Douglass and the Constraints of Racialized Writing," in *Frederick Douglass: New Literary and Historical Essays*, ed. Eric J. Sundquist (Cambridge: Cambridge University Press, 1990), pp. 71-72.

4. In Jacobs' narrative, questions of reliability are not unwarranted. In her own preface, Jacobs [Brent] claims immediately: "Reader be assured this narrative is no fiction.... I have not exaggerated the wrongs inflicted by Slavery [sic]; on the contrary, my descriptions fall far short of the facts" (p. xiii).

"Brent's" narrative was originally introduced by L. Maria Child, in which she admits to some judicious tampering: "At her [Brent's] request I revised her manuscript; but changes as I have made have been mainly for purposes of condensation and orderly arrangement. I have not added any thing [sic] to the incidents, or changed the import of her very pertinent remarks. With trifling exceptions, both the ideas and the language are her own. I pruned excrescences a little, but otherwise I had no reason for changing her lively and dramatic way of telling her own story. The names of both persons and places are known to me; but for good reasons I suppress them" (p. xi).

In her preface to another edition of this work, Jean Fagan

Yellin admits that she once dismissed *Incidents* "as a false slave narrative." Yellin says she changed her mind because she later learned that the abolitionist press had once pulled a false narrative [Yellin does not identify it, but it could James Williams' fraudulent narrative, which began serialization in Feb. 1835], thereby making Yellin more confident that Child's editing was only that. See the Preface to Jacobs' *Incidents in the Life of a Slave Girl*, ed. Jean Fagan Yellin (Cambridge: Harvard University Press, 1987), p. vii.

The whole question of slave narratives' reliability is debated in Houston Baker's *The Journey Back* (Chicago: University of Chicago Press, 1980). There, Baker takes an intensive look at Booker T. Washington's *Up From Slavery* (pp. 46-52). Baker points out that Washington's claim that the Klu Klux Klan was no longer a threat was a blatant falsehood. Furthermore, Baker argues about such works that:

> If it [*Up From Slavery*] falsifies details of the journey, it promises much for our understanding of the voyage into language....
>
> The culturally unique aspects of *Up From Slavery* reside, ... at a level of functional oppositions. In this case, the disparity is between a graphically depicted hell of rural, impoverished, illiterate black southern life and an intriguingly displayed heaven of black southern urbanity, thrift, and education. Two distinct modes of discourse sustain this opposition--the autobiographical self exists in the former, while the fictive self lives in (and testifies to the possibility of) the latter. (p. 52)

5. The gender option of flight versus remaining with the family persists as a theme in modern African American novels, as shall be discussed in Chapter Four of this work.

6. *Blues, Ideology, and Afro-American Literature: A Vernacular Theory* (Chicago: University of Chicago Press, 1984), p. 52.

7. Ibid.

8. Ibid., p. 55.

9. *Passing* (Salem, NH: Ayer, 1986); *Not Without Laughter* (New York: Collier Books, 1969); *Sula* (New York: Plume, 1982). Any subsequent references to these novels will be denoted by page number in parentheses.

10. (New York: Pocket Books, 1986). All subsequent citations of this novel are of this edition and will be denoted by page number in parentheses.

11. *The Street* (Boston: Beacon Press, 1985). All subsequent references to this novel are to this edition and are denoted by page number in parentheses.

12. By romanticizing the blues, I refer particularly to Langston Hughes' *Not Without Laughter* (1930). In that work, the story's cynosure, Sandy, is, at novel's end, able to go to college thanks to his blues singing sister, Harriett, whose success affords her the ability to send her young brother. I consider this happy ending a romanticization of the blues, especially the implication that the talented blues artist is assured of success and, likewise, will feel a commitment to family and race. The following dialogue also exemplifies what I have called romanticization in its elevated, idealistic language:

[Harriett]: "...He's [Sandy] gotta be what his grandma Hager wanted him to be--able to help the black race, Annjee! You hear me? Help the whole race!"

"I want to," Sandy said. (p. 303)

13. Dorson, ed., *Folklore and Folklife: An Introduction* (Chicago: University of Chicago Press, 1972), p. 21.

14. *The Uses of Enchantment: The Meaning and Importance of Fairy Tales* (New York: Knopf, 1976), pp. 4-9.

15. Introduction to *Uncle Remus: His Songs and His Sayings* (New York: Penguin Books, 1982), p. 25.

16. "The Failure of Folklore in Richard Wright's *Black Boy*," *Journal of American Folklore* 104, no. 431 (summer 1991): p. 275.

17. "The Art of Fiction: *An Interview*," in *The Black Novelist*, ed. Robert Hemenway (Columbus, OH: Charles E. Merrill Publishing Co., 1970), p. 213.

18. Deborah E. McDowell, "The Self in Bloom: Alice Walker's *Meridian*," *College Language Association Journal* 24 (March 1981): p. 262.

19. "Identity in the Work of Alice Walker," *College Language Association Journal* 23 (summer 1979): p. 91.

20. "Feminism and the Fairy Tale," in *Making Connections Across the Curriculum: Reading for Analysis*, ed. Patricia Chittenden, et. al. (New York: St. Martin's Press, 1986): p. 632. Reprint of article of same name in *Women's Studies* 6 (1979): pp. 237-57.

21. Peter Erickson, "Identity in the Work of Alice Walker," Ibid., p. 91.

22. Martha J. McGowan, "Atonement and Release in Alice Walker's *Meridian*," *Critique* 23, no. 1 (1981): p. 31.

23. Deborah E. McDowell, Ibid., p. 264, fn 9.

24. Meridian speculates that Raymond's marriage to a dark-skinned woman is racially motivated (p. 111); the motivation for Truman's marriage to Lynne (and Tommy Odd's rape of Lynne) are clouded by numerous references to the race issue.

25. Both Meridian and Lynne are initially sexually involved with Truman, who bounces back and forth between them. But in the second section of the novel, both women lose their mothers' love because of their refusal to submit to their respective culture's expectations of them. Both also recognize consciously that despite their suffering, they are lucky to have realized an opportunity for "choice": Meridian reflects that unlike herself, her female ancestors "had not lived in an age of choice" (p. 124); Lynne says to Meridian, "Because of him [Truman], I can never be as dumb as my mother was" (p. 181). And finally, clouds of guilt encumber both women: for examples of Meridian's guilt see pp. 51, 91, 96, and others; for examples of Lynne's see pp. 133, 159, and 181.

26. Deborah E. McDowell, Ibid., p. 266.

27. *Celebration of Life: Studies in Modern Fiction* (New York: Sheed & Ward, 1972), p. 67.

28. *The Hero With A Thousand Faces*, Second Edition (Princeton: Princeton University Press, 1968), pp. 245-46.

III

THE MILITANT MULE:
ALICE WALKER'S *THE COLOR PURPLE*

In Alice Walker's *The Color Purple* and Zora Neale Hurston's *Their Eyes Were Watching God*,[1] the central characters, Celie and Janie, respectively, grow from young girls whose destinies are ruled and defined by men, into women who control their own lives. What makes these women's success remarkable is that each begins her climb from the bottom rung of a society which promulgates the believe that women are "the mules of the world." Esteemed so little, these women, and those close to them, lead lives of desperation and are the frequent victims of rape, beatings, and emotional and spiritual abuse. Hurston's work was a major influence on Walker;[2] it is not surprising, therefore, that their works would explore common themes, particularly the sexual oppression of women.[3]

It is also not surprising that Hurston's collections of African American folklore should inspire Walker. Indeed, both authors' works reflect a common faith in the cultural value and integrity of African American dialect, and their characters reflect that belief.[4] Furthermore, in the works of both women, folk traditions and folk tales provide a significant part of their characters' cultural heritage. For instance, a belief in hoodoo and the powers of a woman's curse can explain the precipitous death of Jody in Hurston's novel and Albert's dramatic personality change in Walker's novel--both instances in which an otherwise satisfactory explanation is lacking. Despite this common ground, some very significant differences arise when examining how each author explored, in the novels under consideration, strategies for

51

women to overcome sexual oppression at the hands of men. Even conceding the fact that Hurston's *Their Eyes Were Watching God* antedates *The Color Purple* by forty-five years, thereby effectively restricting the "realistic" options available to Janie in the rebellion against male-oppression, Hurston still chooses the option of flight for Janie--a rather timeless choice, yet one that is also clearly evasive.[5] Walker, on the other hand, opts to explore Celie's life *within* the context of a community. In a dramatic context arguably more relevant, *The Color Purple* addresses the real problems women (and men) face *within their* community and suggests ways to correct those problems *within that community.*

In her essay "Domestic Violence in Literature," Ruth Nadelhaft traced images of domestic violence in literature from *Othello* to *The Color Purple.* Interestingly, she concluded that before *The Color Purple*, "Earlier writers about domestic violence have regularly shown that the preservation of the self has demanded the dissolution of a relationship or the literal destruction of the abusive husband. It has been impossible, until now, for a writer to imagine the circumstances in which the beaten wife might recreate her self and the self of the man who beats [her],...." *The Color Purple*, Nadelhaft goes on to say, "does not evade, but tries to solve [these] problems."[6] With few reservations, I think Nadelhaft's thesis is correct, especially when contrasting *Their Eyes Were Watching God* and *The Color Purple*, as this essay will briefly do.[7]

In *Their Eyes Were Watching God*, Janie neither confronts her problems nor does she confront her husbands directly: she runs off with Jody to flee Logan Killocks; later, she curses Jody, who dies, and moves on with Tea Cake in order to avoid Eatonville's scorn. For Janie, whose eyes are always on the horizon, the answer to her dilemmas is avoidance and/or flight. I would be quick to add that Janie never questions directly the wisdom of the institutions which confine and restrict her. Rather than act, Janie reacts. And with her men, she allows herself to be defined by either the limits they impose, or the freedoms they grant. Ultimately, although Janie Mae Crawford-Killocks-Starks-(Tea Cake) matures into a woman clearly different from the sisterhood of Eatonville, because of her acts of flight, her victory is too personal, too internalized, and too socially isolated--despite the fact that Phoeby Watson will surely retell Janie's story--for her experiences to serve as a realistic and accessible social model for other woman to copy--except at the symbolic level. In addition, Hurston's men are static; they do not change through their experience with Janie. They are either insensitive to her needs and desires as Logan and Jody are, or they are already "liberated" as Tea Cake is. In Hurston's vision, in a world in which men do not change, women face only two alternatives: lives of relentless desperation or flight.

On the other hand, despite important similarities with Janie, Walker's Celie differs from Janie in one major and fundamental way: Celie remains committed to her community. She does not flee it. Instead, Celie's story suggests that it is possible *within* their community for women to find and provide for one another the models and the mutual assistance necessary to overcome what is the major demon of both Walker's and Hurston's novels: sexual oppression. The first step towards this realization is, in both novels, for the women to dissociate from men. Thus, while Janie flees her oppressors (with what she hopes are better men), Celie, who remains in her community, *writes* as a way of preserving a sense of self. Thus we find that from the novel's onset, Celie neither assumes for herself, nor reveals in her letters, the surname of the male characters with whom she lives.[8] Defining herself as just "Celie," Celie thus maintains a sense of her own identity, and at least a symbolic detachment from the men in her life. This may seem heroic to some degree, except that for Celie the process of dissociation goes to an extreme. For while Celie's detachment from men suggests that she has retained at least a grain of self-worth and self-respect, the reader will realize that except for Nettie and "God," Celie has, as a defensive reaction to her abuse, detached herself from everything earthly-- including men, women, and nature. Only after Shug's arrival in Celie's life, does Celie's ensuing sexual and spiritual development evolve enough to allow her reassociation with the world of women, and the greater world that is nature. Significantly, because Celie's reassociation with the world becomes a matter of public display, she is able to inspire the other male-dominated women in the novel; thus her growth is reflected in the simultaneous growth of Squeak and Nettie. Just as importantly, in Walker's portrayal of the oppressive evils of patriarchy, even the men are given enough attention to dramatize their own growth; thus, Albert finds it necessary to change in order to find peace with himself and to live happily as a member of the community. Thus, unlike Janie, Celie's rise in self-esteem offers a more accessible and complete model for the other women in the novel and, as important, for the men.

One of Walker's aims--and here she surpasses Hurston--was to create a community in which black women and men could live mutually nourishing lives, free of sexual stereotypes, for sexual stereotypes are the main demon of *The Color Purple*. As a result, her men are dynamic. Her men grow. And while both sexes accomplish this difficult task of redefining their gender roles within an ostensibly closed community, through the epistolary device of Nettie's letters from Africa (which function to enlarge the scope of the novel's community), Celie's small Georgian community is given more universal significance. This enlargement is the direct result of Nettie's letters which unwittingly provide a means for the reader to discover the folk traditions which both the Olinka tribespeople of Africa and Celie's African American community hold on common.

One of the most valuable lessons learned from Nettie's and Celie's letters and from the novel's folklore is that the road from "mule" to self-reliance is not easy: it is fraught with a number of obstacles, not the least of which are those socially entrenched customs which condone outright the domination of women. For a woman, breaking free of those customs necessarily means confronting the very fabric of her community. Not insignificantly, an integral part of that social fabric is made up of tales and oral traditions which its members freely perpetuate. As necessary to the culture's vitality as that is, folk traditions, including folk customs and tales, can also encourage the sometimes mindless acceptance and perpetuation of sexual stereotypes: the stereotype of the rightfully battered woman; the stereotype of a man righteously empowered to maintain his upper-hand over a woman. In *The Color Purple*, Walker found a way to confront those stereotypes directly and illustrated the possibility of change, thereby avoiding the necessity of flight.

Thadious M. Davis has, I believe correctly, suggested that one of Walker's strategies in *The Color Purple* was to use stereotypes to define her male characters. Concerning Walker's presentation of men, Davis comments:

> Walker first depicts what has come to be the stereotypes of blacks, essentially those set destructive patterns of emotional and psychological responses of black men to black life, their women, children, friends, whites, and themselves. Then she loosens the confines of the stereotype and attempts to penetrate

the nexus of feelings that make these lives valuable in themselves and for others.[9]

A similar claim can be made of Walker's depiction of women. The women of *The Color Purple* are also based on stereotypes found not only in the everyday vernacular, but also within African American folklore. Like Hurston, Walker invokes folk tales as a means of explaining certain common cultural perceptions about gender roles; but Walker didn't stop there in *The Color Purple*. Walker's use of African American folklore was also ironic. In Walker's novel, the use of folklore becomes a fundamental way of illustrating the destructive and dangerously counterproductive implications of gender roles, especially for women.[10] A case in point is the folk tale "Why the Sister in Black Works Hardest," a tale collected by Hurston and printed in her *Mules and Men*:

> Know how it happened? After God got thru makin' de world and de varmints and de folks, he made up a great big bundle and let it down in de middle of de road. It laid dere for thousands of years, the Ole Missus said to Ole Massa: "Go pick up dat box, Ah want to see whut's in it." Ole Massa look at de box and it look so heavy dat he says to de nigger, "Go fetch me dat big ole box out dere in de road." De nigger been stumblin' over de box a long time so tell his wife:
> "'Oman, go git dat box." So the nigger 'oman she runned to git de box. She says:
> "Ah always lak to open up a big box 'cause there's nearly always something good in great big boxes." So she run and grabbed a-hold of de box and opened it up and it was full of hard work.
> Dat's the reason de sister in black works harder than anybody else in de world. De white man tells de nigger to work and he takes and tells his wife.[11]

An abbreviated version of this tale also appears in *Their Eyes Were Watching God*, and immediately precedes Janie's Grandma's proclamation that "the nigger woman is de mule uh de world..." (p. 16). What this tale illustrates is a dangerous bias and a social hierarchy which operates within the African American world view: while portraying the black male as inferior to whites (remembering, of course, that this is a slavery tale), it also contends that the black male is superior to the black woman. The dangers such tales promulgate for black women should be obvious: the black woman is stereotyped, as Janie' grandmother claimed, as her culture's "mule"; further, that role is given credibility and the weight of authority because it appears to have stood the test of time, and, ostensibly, because God set the process in motion, appears to have His approval. If there's a top, there must be a bottom, and the African American woman is it.

In *Their Eyes Were Watching God*, Hurston utilized this folk motif effectively, harnessing it to the theme of "black woman as mule." Thus, we note that Janie is not blind to the significance of being literally teemed with a mule: when Logan Killocks goes off "tuh buy a mule Fuh me tuh plow" (p. 27), Janie realizes that Logan's days of honeymooning and kissing her feet are over, and so she flees with Jody Starks. But later as "Mrs. Mayor," trapped under the domineering and socially conscious thumb of Joe, Janie is treated with the same degree of insensitivity that Matt Bonner treats his yellow, underfed, and over-worked mule. The fact that Joe can and does buy Bonner's mule, combined with the spectacle of Joe's mock-eulogy for the mule, during which Joe speaks from atop the dead mule's distended stomach, further illustrates the complete domination of the black male over his mule-mate. The result: Janie ultimately flees once again to escape sexual oppression; but even with Tea Cake, Janie is bound to a migratory lifestyle.

In *The Color Purple*, Walker is also careful to draw Celie's relationship to Mr.___ in terms that suggest Celie is a beast of burden:

> Mr.___ pick up a hoe and start to chop. He chop bout three chops then he don't chop again. He drop the hoe in the furrow, turn right back on his heel, walk back to the house, go git him a cool drink of water, git his pipe, sit on the porch and stare. I follow cause I think he sick. Then he say, You better git on back to the field. Don't wait for me. (p. 26)

The theme of woman as mule is developed more directly later in the novel when Nettie writes to Celie describing the relationship between the Olinka chief and his wives. "Even though they are unhappy and work like *donkeys* they still think it is an honor to be the chief's wife"

(p. 133, emphasis added). Additionally, near the novel's close, Albert and Celie are speaking about Celie's telling Shug that Albert beat her. Albert says: "I know it, he say, and I don't blame you. If a *mule* could tell folk how its treated, it would" (p. 229; emphasis added).[12] In both novels, the authors, through dialogue, letters, and analogy, harness their central females to "the mule" not only as a means of establishing their characters' lowness, but also in real terms binding both Janie and Celie to the folk tradition of "Why the Sister in Black Works Hardest." The purpose of this is to provide the reader with a sharp and powerful contrast against which to gauge and judge the characters' later development.

Despite Alice Walker's debt to Zora Neale Hurston, and to folklore, it seems clear that Walker realized that any writer who allowed her work to remain bound by the tenets of folklore would find herself trapped by their moral precepts. In *The Color Purple*, Walker was looking for a way, while acknowledging the blacks' collective debt to folk tradition, to transcend folklore's limitations. Celie's triumph was due in great part to her breaking free of traditional roles and intellectual perceptions, and then redefining both *what she was* and *what God was*. Paradoxically, Walker discovered the key to solving this riddle in the stockpile of Hurston-collected folk tales. I refer to another folk tale collected in *Mules and Men*. Too long to cite in toto, I offer this summary:

In the beginning, God made man and woman equal, including physical strength. Man got tired of fighting and not winning, so he asked God for more strength than woman. His wish was granted. Woman, not liking the beating she gets as a result, goes to God and asks for the same gift. God refuses her request, so woman "went straight to the devil" and was advised by the devil to ask for the bunch of keys God kept on His mantle. God gave them to woman; and the devil told woman how to use them. He said the keys are to "de kitchen," "de bedroom," and to "de cradle and he [man] don't want to be cut off from his generations at all."[13]

This tale of the three keys, while underscoring the apparently ages-old tension that has existed between the sexes, implies a number of disturbing things: first, that although men and women were created equal long-ago, that is no longer true; second, that God played an active and conscious role in bestowing upon man the physical prowess to beat and dominate women; third, that women might be able to live under the conditions of an uneasy truce if they can learn to cleverly wield "their keys." Walker knew this tale well; and I believe that three of her major female characters in *The Color Purple* were molded to represent women who stood at different levels of this power struggle.

At the pinnacle of this power struggle stands Shug Avery. She is woman in possession of a disarming set of keys: she is beautiful, sexy, talented, independent, and by the novel's end, wealthy. As the novel's most complete portrait of an uncompromised woman, Shug is the woman who can help Celie achieve her independence and develop her self-esteem. The dexterity with which she manipulates Albert, while preserving her autonomy, makes Shug a paradigm of the empowered black woman.

Sofia is the novel's most tragic figure. One of a tribe of proud Amazon-like warriors, she is Walker's atavistic version of the "three keys" "first" woman: a woman pugnacious and strong-willed, proud and defiant, willing and able to slug it out toe-to-toe with Harpo and, mistakenly, the mayor. Sofia's pride and dignity earn our respect; but her inability to compromise or to curb her pride prove to be the flaw which brings ruin to her life. It is ironic perhaps that Harpo's desire to dominate Sofia provides the novel with one of its few truly comic subplots--his gluttonous drive to gain weight as a way of gaining physical superiority over Sofia. Together, both Sofia and Harpo give flesh and blood to the nameless first woman and man of the "three keys" folk tale.[14]

Coming finally to the character of Celie, one is tempted to remark: last but not least. The pathetic truth is, however, Celie was both last and least. No one in the novel is quite so low as Celie as a young girl. She was repeatedly victimized and raped by Pa; her two babies were stolen from her; even her ability to bear children withered up and left her barren. "I don't bleed no more" she writes (p. 7). When, later in the novel, Celie confides to Shug: "I'm pore, I'm black, I may be ugly and can't cook..." (p. 176), it is unequivocally clear just how vulnerable and powerless Celie has been during her life. In terms of the folk tale under consideration, Celie lacked every key which it was her right as a woman to possess. She admits she can't cook (the key to "de kitchen"); she is sexually abused on the one hand and, on the other, she is sexually dormant before her relationship with Shug (the key to "de bedroom"); and because she lacks the power of reproduction, she forfeits the key to "de generations." Without a single key to defend herself, Celie is placed in the world of men as naked as a motherless child.

In *The Color Purple*, Walker developed a hierarchy of women who reflected the social spectrum, each with a firm link to folk tradition. This strategy places her women within the context of their native folk traditions and community. Through contrast, Walker was also able to provide her women models and strategies for survival. Further, this hierarchy allowed Walker to dramatize the breadth and width of Celie's triumph by contrasting the lowness and smallness of her early life with her increasing involvement in an ever-broadening community of women, her growing sense of self-worth, and her deepening spiritual awareness.

Having linked Celie to the folk traditions of "the Sister in Black" ("woman as mule") and "the three keys," the novel moves to break those restraints, to ultimately transcend them, and thus to propose to Celie's folk community that it is possible for black women (and men) to live together productively and in harmony.

Walker's central plot in *The Color Purple* is clear: it is Celie's role to overturn and transcend the anachronistic folk traditions of her community and, while still firmly rooted in them, suggest new modes of living. But before Celie can develop the self-confidence to challenge God's order and authority, she must develop the confidence and capability to confront man's authority. Celie takes this initial step unwittingly as she finds herself in love with first the "idea" of Shug Avery (p. 8), and then with Shug herself. Thereafter, Celie finds the power and protection she needs to continue her process of personal growth.

Celie's growth has several ramifications, not the least of which is the way she perceives the world, and the changing way in which Celie's community sees her. This process of change can be illustrated in the novel's development of the following motifs: the way Celie perceives other people; in the changing ways the woman in Celie's community support one another; in the way Celie perceives God and nature, particularly trees; Celie's sexual awakening; and, in the breakdown of traditional sex roles. The remainder of this chapter will examine those motifs.

Celie's lowness: Having earlier illustrated in this paper the roots of the "woman as mule" stereotype in *The Color Purple*, it shouldn't be difficult to recognize that after a lifetime of such treatment a woman's view of herself and others would reflect that impression. Celie is no exception. Her early letters to God reflect her sense of worthlessness, her lowness, and the absence of spirit in others.

Celie writes of Mr.___: "He look at me. It like he looking at the earth" (p. 20). In order to harden herself against pain, Celie's solution is to "make myself wood" (p. 22). Of Harpo, Celie reflects, "Patting Harpo back not even like patting a dog. It more like patting another piece of wood. Not a living tree, but a table, a chifferobe" (p. 29). When Celie sees Sofia the first time, her impression is that Sofia's skin gleams like "good furniture" (p. 30). The most degrading image is related in Celie's conversation with Shug about having sex with Mr.___. Shug remarks: "Do his business. Why, Miss Celie. You make it sound like he going to the toilet on you"; to which Celie responds: "That what it feel like, I say" (p. 68). For Celie, the world, the people, and the things that occupy it are spiritless, nearly lifeless, objects. In the eyes of her Pa, Celie was unfit to educate (p. 9). Even Celie's inability to bear children becomes a selling point in Pa's pitch to unload Celie on Mr.___ (p. 10). (How much like a sterile mule Celie is: you can do anything you want to her and not have to pay for it, Pa implies in his pitch to unload Celie!) Before Mr.___ decides to accept Pa's offer, he asks to see Celie, and the scene of Celie turning around to give a full view of her body, while Mr.___ reviews her from his horse, recalls the degrading spectacle of a slave or animal auction block (p. 12).

Once in Mr.___'s house, Celie's degraded self-image is obvious to a growing number of women. They advise Celie to assert herself, to fight back. Nettie tells Celie to fight Mr.___'s children in order to gain the upper hand. "You got to fight them, Celie, she say. I can't do it for you. You got to fight them for yourself" (p. 21). Sofia's advice to Celie about Mr.___ is predictable. "You ought to bash Mr.___ head open, she say" (p. 39). Celie's reaction to Sofia's advice is to laugh. To Nettie's advice, Celie's reaction is more revealing: "I don't say nothing. I think about Nettie, dead. She fight, she run away. What good it do? I don't fight, I stay where I'm told. But I'm alive" (p. 21).

Celie may be "alive," but that's the sum total of all she is until Shug Avery enters her life. The introduction of Shug to the novel finally gives Celie something worth living for--first Shug, and then herself. The key to this discovery is sex and sexuality. Ironically, the very qualities which make women vulnerable, and have been the source of Celie's greatest pain, are also the keys to Celie's liberation. Through Celie's intimate relationship with Shug, Celie discovers the powers of her own sexuality and begins to awaken to the spirituality of life and nature. Love is not only a tonic, it is a baptism which bestows new life to Celie's spirit and intellect.

Signalling Celie's personal awakening is the poignant scene in which Shug unfolds the mysteries and pleasures of the "button" (p. 69). This scene in isolation might seem mildly comic. But when later recalled in light of the Olinka female initiation ceremony, Celie's discovery of sexual gratification through use of her "button" makes this scene intensely ironic. While in Africa this ritual of mutilation affirms the rights of men to control women in the most cruel and selfish of ways, Celie's awakening to her sexuality spurs her rejection of everything that maleness stands for: possession, sexual lust, and domestic servitude.

The union between sex and spirit, the physical and the spiritual, provides the spark that ignites Celie's rebellion against first the men who have oppressed her and then God. Thus, as if Shug had resuscitated her, the immediate results of Celie's sexual flowering are that she begins to feel truly alive. "My life stop when I left home, I think. But then I think again. It stop with Mr.___ maybe, but start up again with Shug" (p. 72). This life-giving bond between Celie and Shug is sealed when the two women begin to sleep together habitually (p. 96). This event marks a major transition in the novel's plot, for it announces that Celie has finally acquired some degree of autonomy and power. In terms of the "three keys" motif, Celie's and Shug's mutual love gives to Celie her first "key": the key to the bedroom and a sex life without compromise. Swiftly following, Shug gets her hands on a single letter from Nettie. Reading it, Celie discovers that not only is Nettie alive and safe, but so too are her children (p. 100). Celie thus acquires her second "key": the key to her generations and her family. The critic

Thadious Davis noted the significance of "generations" not only in *The Color Purple*, but also in other of Walker's works. She writes:

> The achievements and dreams that emerge from the connected experience of generations are expressions of freedom and beauty, of power and community. The primary dream ... is that of freedom to be one's own self, specifically to be one's own black self and to claim ... one's own life for one's self and for future generations.[15]

Celie's personal odyssey continues as, with Shug's help, Celie uncovers a packet of letters from Nettie in Mr.___'s trunk. After reading both the single letter and the bundle, a once battered Celie is seized by an urge to kill Mr.___. After reading the first letter from Nettie, Celie writes, "I watch him close, I begin to feel a lightening in the head. Fore I know anything I'm standing hind his chair with his razor open" (p. 102). After devouring the bundle from the trunk, Celie says to Shug, "How I'm gon keep from killing him" (p. 122).

Despite Celie's rage, she does not kill Mr.___; but the image of a sharp razor held close to his neck (ironically signifying the image of the razor used in the Olinka female initiation ceremony) signals a cleaving, a change in Celie that is permanent. In terms of the knife's thematic significance--who wields the knife and for what purpose--this point represents a dramatic overturning of the novel's power structure, from men to women. From that point on in the novel, strengthened by the knowledge that she has "generations," Celie has the fortitude and courage to pursue her own independence. What follows immediately thereafter in the novel is the birth of the "folkpants" concept, which is the key to Celie's economic independence (her successful negotiation of the economics of slavery); also, there is Celie's confession that her relationship with Shug isn't totally satisfying, signally the beginnings of her understanding that she will some day need to live on her own (p. 124).

Friendship among women: The love between Celie and Shug broadens to include other women. As Celie realizes a growing sense of personal value, so too do the women around her. One of the novel's major themes is that women need to help women, or as Celie says early in the novel, "I don't even look at mens. That's the truth. I look at woman,..." (p. 7).

In her discussion of *The Color Purple*, Ruth Nadelhaft remarks that "women are each other's source of strength.... There is a tradition of cooperation among these beaten blacks, an awareness out of history that they must give to one another."[16] And yet, as we might expect, Walker's portrayal of woman helping women is not always uplifting. Early in the novel the occasions when women aid other women frequently are the result of duress, are performed in an environment of coercion such that the women are compelled to sacrifice (even if willingly) their dignity to appease the lust of men. For example, Celie in an act of genuine love and compassion, acts as a decoy sacrificing herself to save Nettie from Pa's unmitigated lust (pp. 5,7,9,). Squeak, utilizing the folk strategy of a Brer Rabbit trickster tale, allows herself to be raped in order to help Sofia get transferred out of prison and into the mayor's house (pp. 82-84).[17] (This sexual sacrifice is doubly ironic, for Sofia had spent much of her life fending off incestuous assaults in her own home (p. 38); Squeak's sexual sacrifice emboldens her to the point that she demands to be called by her more dignified name, "Mary Agnes" (p. 84), and soon thereafter, embarks on her singing career.) Shug enlists her sexuality for the cause of secretly procuring from Albert, Celie's first letter from Nettie (p. 102).

This network of mutual sacrifice grows even wider as the women assume responsibility for rearing Sofia's children while Sofia is serving time, just as Nettie, through an act of fate is able to serve as Celie's surrogate in Africa. The arms of this "friendship among women," stretching clear across the Atlantic, is commonplace also in the everyday life of the Olinka tribeswomen who "nurse each other's children" selflessly (p. 141).

As mutually nurturing as this sisterhood between women may be, and as necessary, it can also be destructive, for at its heart festers the need for women to compromise themselves because they are denied any other avenue of power when confronting or dealing with men. What this system produces in Africa is women who "cannot look in a man's face.... They look instead at his feet or his knees" (p. 137). In Africa, this system also creates males who ignore their mothers after they reach manhood, and, in America, children who are stripped from their mothers and thus neither recognize nor love them (as in Sofia's and Celie's case).

All hope is not lost however. Just as Celie's lowness provides contrast to her later development, so too Walker proposes that women can benefit one another productively, without falling victim to dehumanizing demands in the process. In a scene that is one of the novel's climaxes--the dinner scene--Celie reads Mr.___ the riot act, Squeak makes her declaration of independence from Harpo, and Sofia, aghast at the changes going on springs back to life and vows to care for Suzie Q in Squeak's absence (pp. 169-74). Shug, of course, is the unselfish catalyst spurring these women into action and independence. The shocked and dumbfounded menfolk, Mr.___ and Harpo, respond characteristically by name-calling, proclaiming death threats, then change to the subtler ploys of the comforts of home and the economics of the purse strings. But by then it's too late. The women have overcome the economics of slavery and are ready to live autonomous, self-defined lives.

Redefining "GOD": Of Sofia, Squeak, and Shug, the novel has little more to say; for them, the process of growth and change climaxes during the dinner scene. Sofia settles into homemaking again with a gentler Harpo; Squeak embarks on her singing career; and Shug's central role begins to pale in comparison to the spiritual emergence of Celie.

For Celie, the shock that brings her face-to-face with her perceptions of God is the letter from Nettie which reveals the secrets of her parentage and heritage (pp. 148-50). Celie's response is unnerving: "My daddy lynch. My mama crazy. All my little half-brothers and sisters no kin to me. My children not my sister and brother. Pa not pa. You [God] must be sleep" (p. 151). Celie's first visible reaction to this "family" news is to immediately begin addressing her letters to Nettie, not God, marking a signal moment in the novel. For Celie has somehow made the intellectual connection between the maleness of man (Pa) and the maleness of God. In Celie's patriarchal world, she recognized that if the man she had called her Pa all her life (as a matter of faith) was not really her pa, then by analogy, perhaps it is also true that God is not God. Celie's doubts about the nature of God surface in a conversation with Shug and are recorded in another letter to Nettie:

Dear Nettie,

    I don't write to God no more, I write to you.

    What happen to God? ast Shug.

    Who that? I say.

    She look at me serious.

    Big a devil as you is, I say, you not worried bout no God, surely.

    She say, Wait a minute. Hold on just a minute here. Just because I don't harass it like some peoples us know don't mean I ain't got religion.

    What God do for me? I ast.

    She say, Celie! Like she shock. He gave you life, good health, and a good woman that love you to death.

    Yeah, I say, and he give me a lynched daddy, a crazy mama, a lowdown dog of a step pa and a sister I probably won't ever see again. Anyhow, I say, the God I been praying and writing to is a man. And act just like all the other mens I know. Trifling, forgitful and lowdown.

    She say, Miss Celie. You better hush. God might hear you.

    Let 'im hear me, I say. If he ever listened to poor colored women the world would be a different place, I can tell you. (p. 164)

At this point in the novel, Celie's confidence in herself is so strong that she is not only capable of questioning man's authority over her, but God's; she has also succeeded in rejecting them for something more immediate and satisfying.

    The supplanting of a heavenly God for a more tangible, visible earthly divinity is the result of Celie's growing affection for nature generally, but most specifically for trees.[18] Like so many of the themes in *The Color Purple*, once Celie's awareness blossoms, we are able to contrast Celie's earlier impressions with her later ones. As a symbol for the oneness of nature, Celie's depiction and identification with trees, therefore, changes and becomes more spiritual in concert with the growth of her own self-esteem and complexity.

    At first trees are only lifeless wood, but because they are also strong and silent, they, like Celie, are able to withstand the beatings of mankind. "I make myself wood. I say to myself, Celie, you a tree.

That's how come I know trees fear man" (p. 22). Harpo is like a piece of wood to Celie (p. 42); Sofia's skin is like the shine on "good furniture" (p. 30); and Squeak "smell like a good clean floor" (p. 82). In these unsettling descriptions of people, trees and wood have been reduced to objects, the products of man; taken in the context of the novel, the metaphors are demeaning and degrading, the people described perceived as further extensions of man's (the male's) ability to manipulate nature.

But with Shug Avery, even early in the novel, Celie perceives that trees can be as potentially alive and receptive to beauty as Celie is. "She [Shug] look so stylish it like the trees all around the house draw themselves up for a better look" (p. 42). A letter from Nettie which recounts the Olinka folk tale about the symbiotic relationship between the Olinka and the roofleaf concludes with the words of the tribesman Joseph: "We know roofleaf is not Jesus Christ, but in its own humble way, is it not God?" (p. 131). Shug, in the conversation with Celie in which Celie calls God "lowdown," later reflects a sentiment similar to the Olinka's: "She say, My first step from the old white man [God] was trees. Then air. Then birds. Then other people. But one day ... I know that if I cut a tree, my arm would bleed' (p. 167). Appropriately, Shug-the-life-giver, has a house with "lots of trees around it" (p. 177).

According to Judeo-Christian tradition, God is not only all-powerful, He also metes out justice. But by the time Celie curses Mr.___, Celie has so little faith left in those assumptions that she turns to nature's authority, instead of God's, for the power to curse Mr.___. When she curses Mr.___ (in what could be called the novel's indictment of all men, spoken for all women in the voice of Celie), she says: "Until you do right by my, I say, everything you even dream about will fail. I give it to him straight, just like it come to me. And it seem to come to me from the trees" (p. 176).[19]

In her apotheosis of nature and trees, Celie has successfully broken free of the constraints of the folk group she shares, and which generally perceives and accepts the Judeo-Christian God/man/woman-as-mule hierarchy as ordained. Trudier Harris, in an article dealing with the folk and humanism, remarks that Christianity has never really espoused the ideals of blacks. She writes:

> I maintain that religion--here Christianity specifically--
> did and does not embody the values many Black folk wanted
> to preserve. When the choice is between Christian resignation

or faith and humanistic action or reason, literary characters, like their folk counterparts, often reject Christianity in favor of a more exacting and humanistic idealism.... Yet the goals they set for themselves, their aspirations for peace, freedom, and happiness, go beyond Christianity. Here a code of ethics has the folk culture as its basis, although it transcends the limitations of folklore as well.[20]

Androgyny: Celie's emotional and spiritual growth would pale in significance if her triumphs were entirely personal. Unlike Hurston's Janie, Celie's story is only a part of a larger process whose goal it was to suggest that the larger community which enfolds black life is capable of change too. Walker's belief that fiction should be moral [21]--it should teach--compels her to propose one means by which to accomplish both the renewal of and the integration of what is best from our traditions with what is new and enlightened. On the level of community and family, much of Walker's hope lies in the destruction of conventional boundaries which separate and make exclusive the roles the men and women.

What then is the reader to make of Celie's lesbianism? Ultimately, it cannot be perceived as anything more than a personal choice, and then, Walker seems to say, it can only be temporary. Celie seems to voice this position, though she appears confused by her feelings: "Us sleep like sisters, me and Shug. Much as I still want to be with her, much as I love to look, my titties stay soft, my little button never rise" (p. 124). Despite her ambivalent feelings, Celie is reluctant to abandon her intimacy with Shug; thus, it is left to Shug to voice her own needs to end the intimacy and return to heterosexual life. Over Chinese dinner, Shug breaks the news and Celie responds as is her way by writing the unspeakable on a piece of paper and pushing it to Shug (pp. 209-12). (This becomes the only time in the novel that Celie writes to Shug.) Celie suffers over the split, although she had earlier realized the rightness of the male/female sexual bond. Thinking of Mr.___ and Shug, Celie wrote: "He love looking at Shug. I love looking at Shug. But Shug don't love looking at but one of us. Him. But that the way it spose to be. I know that. But if that so, why my heart hurt me so?" (p. 64).

The solution to this puzzle of sexual roles, Walker outlines, is the same as the solution to the puzzle that keeps God so removed from man: the definitions, the delineations that separate men and women must be broken down and discarded; they must be retailored, let-out, enlarged enough to clothe both sexes in the same garment.

One of Walker's earliest hints of this refashioning was to alternately describe both Celie and Shug as "men." When Celie bathes Shug, Celie's reaction is startlingly uncharacteristic: "First time I got the full sight of Shug Avery long black body with it black plum nipples, look like her mouth, I thought I had turned into a man" (p. 45). Later, Celie astutely comments on the occasional manliness of Shug: "That when I notice how Shug talk act sometimes like a man" (p. 72). Shug, using a courting ploy that recalls Hurston's Jody and Tea Cake, woos Celie by conjuring visions of a better life: "If you was my wife, she say, I'd cover you up with kisses, and work for you too" (p. 95). These androgynous motifs crop up elsewhere as well. In fact, the first time in her life Celie is conscious of feeling contented is when she, Shug, and, surprisingly, Mr.___ are all engaged in the womanly folk art of quilting (p. 52).[22] And, Celie's economic independence is, of course, the result of her unisex "folkpants."

If the destruction of the traditional definitions of male and female roles is necessary for the healthy and mutually beneficial propagation of the African American culture, as Celie's story affirms, then we have to ask who is to serve as the black culture's new model? Walker is bold enough to suggest that the answer somehow lies in the "generations," and in redefining the role of tradition. Shug Avery, so ideal a model of independence for Celie, is ultimately too footloose, too distant from her own children, to serve in this capacity. Celie alone is not fit; nor would Celie and Albert together, even after his "rebirth." Regrettably, Nettie and Samuel's marriage--the one mating in the novel which appears truly blissful--comes too late in their lives to serve either.

Walker's hopes lies in two minor characters. They are Tashi and Adam, an Olinka woman and an African/American male, who also happens to be Celie's son. Together, their marriage suggests a blending of African tradition with American life. Tashi's female initiation, and Adam's facial scarring, primitive and mutilating as they are, represent not only an affirmation of tradition's significance, but also the hopeful process of cultural blending. For while Tashi's disfigurement (lowness) binds her ritualistically to her African American sisters, Adam's love for Tashi as she is, and his enlightened understanding that the female initiation and all it represents is wrong, makes him the proper bridge and carrier of hope for a new, enlightened African American male. Thadious Davis has voiced a similar opinion:

> Celie's progeny [Adam and Olivia] will make the present and future generations. Their return is cause for a larger hope for the race, and for celebration within the family and community, because they have survived "whole," literally since they miraculously survive a shipwreck and symbolically since they have acquired definite life-affirming attitudes.[23]

Over two centuries ago, Johann Herder claimed that women were victims of subjugation in the "most savage nations throughout the World." He also claimed that: "Most nations that acquire subsistence with difficulty, degrade the female sex to domestic animals, and impose on them all the labours of the hut: the husband imagines bold, manly enterprise sufficiently excuses him from submitting to more trifling occupations, and leaves those to his wife.... The wife of the Negro is far beneath her husband in slavery...."[24] Herder's observation suggests that black women are not uniquely burdened by the problems of oppression and abuse. In our own mid-West, Hamlin Garland's turn-of-the-century stories in *Main-Travelled Roads*, depict the misery of immigrant women who are quite literally teemed with horse or mule in domestic servitude. So too is Antonia, the heroine of Willa Cather's nostalgic *My Antonia*. But, if what Ruth Nadelhaft suggests is valid, and Alice Walker is the first writer to not avoid the issues of domestic violence, either by indirection or avoidance (as in Jacobs' *Incidents* and Hurston's *Their Eyes*), then Walker deserves praise not only for making her characters confront their lives directly, but as an author, for having the courage to face those problems with them.

NOTES

1. *The Color Purple* (New York: Harcourt Brace Jovanovich, Publishers, 1982); *Their Eyes Were Watching God* (1937, Greenwich, CT: Fawcett Publications, 1965). All references to these works will be to these editions are denoted by page numbers in parentheses.

2. For evidence of Hurston's influence on Walker, there are numerous examples, especially in Walker's own *In Search of Our Mothers' Gardens* (New York: Harcourt Brace Jovanovich, Publishers, 1984), especially pp. 3-21, 11-13, 83-92. Walker outright expresses her delight with Hurston's *Mules and Men* and *Their Eyes* on pp. 84-85. Also see John O'Brien's *Interviews With Black Writers* (New York: Liveright, 1973), pp. 200-205.

3. See Hurston's comments about her own birth in *Dust Tracks on a Road: An Autobiography* (1942). She writes that on the occasion of her birth, her father "threatened to cut his throat when he got the news. It seems that one daughter was all that he figured he could stand. My sister, Sarah, was his favorite child, but that one girl was enough. Plenty more sons, but no more girl babies to wear out shoes and bring in nothing. I don't think he ever got over the trick he felt that I played on him by getting born a girl...." (Urbana: University of Illinois Press, 1984), p. 27.

4. Henry Louis Gates' *Signifying Monkey* (New York: Oxford University Press, 1988) claims of *Their Eyes Were Watching God*: "Hurston's text is the first example in our tradition of 'the speakerly text,' by which I mean a text whose rhetorical strategy is designed to represent an oral literary tradition, designed 'to emulate the phonetic, grammatical, and lexical patterns of actual speech and produce the "illusion of oral narration"'" (p. 181). Hurston's novel acknowledges the authenticity and "authority of the black vernacular voice" (p. 183). Most significantly, Gates states that "Hurston showed the tradition just how dialect could blend with standard English to create a new voice, a voice exactly as black as it is white" (p. 251). Of Walker's *The Color Purple*,

Gates says:

"Walker's Signifyin(g) riff on Hurston was to seize upon the device of free indirect discourse as practiced in *Their Eyes* but to avoid standard English almost totally in Celie's narration. Walker has written a novel in dialect, in the black vernacular. The initial impression that we have of Celie's naivete slowly reveals how one can write an entire novel in dialect" (p. 251).

5. Hurston's *Their Eyes* (1937) antedates Petry's *The Street* (1946) by nine years. While Hurston's heroine opts for flight as a strategy against oppression, unlike Lutie Johnson, the heroine of *The Street*, Janie is not a mother.

6. *Mosaic* 17, no. 2 (spring 1984): pp. 254, 257.

7. In *In Search of Our Mothers' Gardens* Walker's comments about Kate Chopin's *The Awakening* echo Nadelhaft's. Not surprisingly, Walker gives Hurston's Janie in *Their Eyes Were Watching God* more credit than I do: "Mme Pontellier, overcome by the strictures of society and the existence of her children (along with the cowardice of her lover), kills herself rather than defy the one and abandon the other. Janie Crawford, on the other hand, refuses to allow society to dictate behavior to her, enjoys the love of a much younger, freedom-loving man, and lives to tell others of her experience" (Ibid., p. 6).

8. Not identifying the name(s) of their slave-owners was a common practice in slave narratives, and certainly has its echoes here. For instance see *Narrative of the Life of Frederick Douglass*, in which Douglass does not reveal the factual names of his owners for fear of causing harm to the slaves left behind. The same is true of Harriet A. Jacobs' slave narrative, *Incidents in the Life or a Slave Girl* (1861), in which she identified herself as "Linda Brent" and also gave fictitious names to persons and places (New York: Harcourt Brace Jovanovich, Publishers, 1973), p. x. See also Hughes and Bontemps' *The Book of Negro Folklore* (1958), wherein a slave narrative utilizes the same convention (New York: Dodd, Mead & Co;, 1983), p. 45. This practice crops up elsewhere too. See Hurston's *Dust Tracks* (Ibid., pp. 134-39) for instance, where Hurston's identifies someone she once knew as "Miss M___."

9. "Alice Walker's Celebration of Self in Southern Generations," *Women Writers of the Contemporary South*, ed. Peggy Whitman Prenshaw (Jackson: University of Mississippi Press, 1984): p. 45.

10. In *Dust Tracks* Hurston also comments on the destructive, counter-productive realities of folklore, especially in "My People! My People!" in which she attacks the retelling of "monkey stories" which defame dark-skinned African Americans (Ibid., pp. 215-37).

11. (Bloomington: Indiana University Press, 1978), pp. 80-81.

12. The connection between the slave and the mule resulted in the word *mulatto*. Literary images which literally portray the negro as mule are rare perhaps, but have been attempted. See Charles Waddell Chesnutt's tale "The Conjurer's Revenge" in *The Conjure Woman*, in which the slave Primus is turned into a mule.

13. Ibid., pp.33-38. Also: A variant form of this folktale can also be found in Hughes and Bontemps' *The Book of Negro Folklore*, Ibid., pp. 130-35.

14. Suggestions of Sofia's character can also be found in other Hurston sources. See Hurston's recollection of her Uncle Jim and Aunt Caroline's fights in *Dust Tracks* (Ibid., pp. 22-25); and Hurston's retelling of Cudjo Lewis' recollection of Amazons sacking his African city, also in *Dust Tracks* (pp. 198-205).

15. Thadius M. Davis, "Alice Walker's Celebration of Self in Southern Generations," *Women Writers of the Contemporary South*, ed. Peggy Whitman Prenshaw (Jackson: University of Mississippi Press, 1984), p. 46.

16. "Domestic Violence in Literature: A Preliminary Study," *Mosaic* 17, no. 2 (spring 1984): p. 255.

17. Tricksters, such as Brer Rabbit, are famous for getting what they want by saying that the thing wanted is the thing not wanted! For examples see Joel Chandler Harris' *Uncle Remus: His Songs and Sayings*, especially "How Mr. Rabbit Was Too Sharp For Mr. Fox" and "Mr. Fox Tackles Old Man Tarrypin," (New York: Penguin, 1982), pp. 62-62, 87-89.

18. Trudier Harris has argued that Walker was familiar with the work of Charles Chesnutt and draws analogies between the authors' uses of folklore--in Chesnutt's *The Conjure Woman* and in Walker's short stories in *In Love & Trouble*. Walker's use of trees in *The Color Purple*, therefore, conjures, somewhat ironically, images of Chesnutt's tale "Po' Sandy," in which the slave Sandy is turned into a tree, but then is cut down and cut up at the planation mill. See, "Folklore in the Fiction of Alice Walker: A Perpetuation of Historical and Literary Traditions," *Black American Literary Forum* 11 (1977): pp. 3-8. Trees are also a

major theme in Hurston's *Their Eyes*. See Henry Louis Gates' discussion of the tree motif in *The Signifying Monkey* (New York: Oxford University Press, 1988), pp. 186-91.

19. The theme of a character's movement away from traditional Christianity and reliance upon Hoodoo and curses was earlier explored by Walker in her short story, "The Revenge of Hannah Kemphuff," one of the stories printed in *In Love & Trouble*.

20. "Three Black Women Writers and Humanism: A Folk Perspective," *Black American Literature and Humanism*, ed. R. Baxter Miller (Lexington: University Press of Kentucky, 1981): p. 52.

21. Walker wrote in *In Search of Our Mothers' Gardens* that "...black writers seem always involved in a moral and/or physical struggle, the result of which is expected to be some kind of larger freedom" (New York: Harcourt Brace Jovanovich, Publishers, 1984), p. 5. Elsewhere in that collection, Walker wrote: "No one could wish for a more advantageous heritage than that bequeathed to the black writer in the South: a compassion for the earth, a trust in humanity beyond our knowledge of evil, and an abiding love of justice. We inherit a great responsibility as well, for we must give voice to centuries not only of silent bitterness and hate but also of neighborly kindness and sustaining love" (p. 21).

22. Creativity and the community of women have always been associated with the arts of weaving, sewing, and quilting. These can be seen in the fairy tales "Sleeping Beauty" and "Rumpelstiltskin"; in Penelope's weaving and unraveling in *The Odyssey*; and in Susan Glaspell's short story "A Jury of Her Peers," in which an observant woman is able to discern clues to a killing as a result of her knowledge of sewing, clues which the sheriff and other men overlook.

23. "Alice Walker's Celebration of Self in Southern Generations," *Women Writers of the Contemporary South*, ed. Peggy Whitman Prenshaw (Jackson: University of Mississippi Press, 1984): p. 52.

24. Johann Gottfried von Herder, "National Genius and the Environment," *Reflections on the Philosophy of the History of Mankind*, ed. and abridged by Frank E. Manuel (Chicago: University of Chicago Press, 1968): p. 63.

IV

ABANDONMENT AND *THE BLUEST EYE*

When James Weldon Johnson's unnamed protagonist in *The Autobiography of an Ex-Colored Man* concluded his narrative with the regret, "I cannot repress the thought that, after all, I have chosen the lesser part, that I have sold my birthright for a mess of pottage," the present day reader may ask what exactly has been "sold"? What about being an African American male in America in 1912, or after, was gratifying? What opportunities has the American experience offered black males? After reading *The Autobiography of an Ex-Colored Man* (1912), *Cane* (1923), *Native Son* (1940), and *Invisible Man* (1952), a reader might surmise: very little.

Each of these novels present male characters who are alienated and whose exercise of power is often perverse. And like the slave narratives written by men, their lives include episodes of flight. In *Ex-Colored Man*, the protagonist seeks refuge, artistic freedom, as well as freedom from his blackness, in Europe. In *Cane*, the story "Blood-Burning Moon" depicts the demise of Tom Burwell, a black man whose misfortune it was to love the same black woman as did the white Bob Stone. When Burwell kills his rival in a knife fight, he flees, is hunted down and is lynched. In *Native Son*, Bigger Thomas, trapped in a white woman's bedroom, inadvertently kills her and, after a period of flight, is caught, jailed, and sentenced to die in the electric chair. The "invisible man" of Ellison's novel, spends much of the novel in flight, ultimately living a life underground. Flight and alienation define the main characters of these works.

Slave histories report that male slaves were much more likely to run away from their masters than females because males were not directly involved in child rearing, might not live with their family, and generally had more knowledge of the world beyond the boundaries of the plantation than did their female counterparts.[1] Although slave narratives went to great lengths to stress the sanctity of the family, as has been discussed in Chapter One, many male slaves found themselves forcibly removed from their kin. As a result, without strong family ties to bind them, men ran away in pursuit of their own freedom virtually unhindered by family or group entanglements. Whether these men found themselves unbound emotionally, or at odds with the power structure of white America, they were free to run. In modern novels, the legacy of flight and abandonment continues to propel male protagonists. Whether this legacy is fed by a primordial call to adventure, political and/or cultural alienation, or by the romantic blues notion of catching the next train out of town, "abandoning" has become a central theme of African American literature.

Characteristically, these alienated males are unmarried (except for the ex-colored man who marries late in the novel), and their search for identity and autonomy is a private and personal pursuit. Are these men modern runaway bondsmen repeating the patterns of flight common before Emancipation, fleeing the political and psychological shackles of a white society which routinely denigrates their sexuality, their families, and their spiritual lives? Or are these men engaged in hero quests?

To explore the possibility that the act of flight (and, therefore, familial abandonment) might somehow fit the archetype of ritualistic initiation (the hero's call to adventure) seems natural. Such a connection, would of course, shed a more positive light on how the flights of these male characters are judged. There are, however, two reasons for not assuming this interpretive stance. The first is that these protagonists do not fit the definition of hero: "the mythic hero by his nature both embodies and transcends the values of his culture."[2] Certainly, the ex-colored man does not embody or transcend the legitimate values of his culture, nor does Bigger Thomas. The second reason these protagonists are not heroic is that although these black males are excluded from partnership in the dominant white culture, they are also alienated from their own African American culture. One need only think of Bigger Thomas' alienation, his refutation of what black life meant to him to understand that he is not heroic in the traditional sense:

He hated his family because he knew that they were suffering and that he was powerless to help them. He knew that the moment he allowed himself to feel to its fullness how they lived, the shame and misery of their lives, he would be swept out of himself with fear and despair.... He knew that the moment he allowed what his life meant to enter fully into his consciousness, he would either kill himself or someone else. So he denied himself and acted tough.[3]

It is the renunciation of their social and cultural condition that protagonists like Bigger embody; because they do not represent African American cultural values, they are neither heroic nor worthy of emulation. What benefit then might a reader gather from these characters' experiences? What positive influence do their stories exert upon the self-image of the African American culture?[4]

Cynthia Davis, commenting on Susan L. Blake's remarks concerning *Invisible Man*, has written that: "Blake suggests that Ellison's 'ritualization' of white brutality--e.g., in the adolescent Battle Royal--suggests a reading--adolescent rites of passage--that contradicts the social reality and almost justifies the event."[5] In contrast, Davis continues, the novels of Toni Morrison avoid:

such a situation by exclusion of whites. White brutality and insensitivity are part of the environment the black characters must struggle with, but they are most often conditions, institutionalized and often anonymous, rather than events with ritualistic overtones. This allows Morrison to focus attention not on the white characters' forcing of mythic rites--as if they were gods--but on the black characters' choices within the context of oppression. In fact, when coercion is exercised by whites in these works, it is as *anti*-mythic. It does not force boys into manhood..., or cause a tragic-hero's cathartic recognition.... It destroys the myth and denies characters entrance in it....[6]

In other words, the literary flight of these males characters, caused as a result of oppression and racism, are not hero journeys from which African American society might expect to receive a boon from a returning, enlightened, hero. These characters do not return. They are lonely, isolated, sometime nameless men whose boon, should they discover a personal one, they are unable to share (especially as a character within the novel), because they lack the foundations of a family and a larger social group. This is a sweeping generalization, certainly; but while conceding that a number of minor contradictions to this thesis no doubt exist, such as the contributions to mankind that these stories make as works of art, the general argument is valid. Because these men are alienated, their stories intensely personal, and because they exist outside the sanctioned limits of their community, they do not serve as models for African American culture.

It should be clear that the four novels under consideration were written about African American men *by African American men*. This point is crucial because abandonment affects both sexes and has become the focus of considerable attention, both structurally and thematically, in the fiction written by African American women, also. Not surprisingly, the conclusions drawn by black women writers on the issue of abandonment differ greatly from that of their male counterparts. Thus, when male writers create characters who grow up fatherless, confused, and ultimately estranged, such as Bigger Thomas or the protagonist in *Ex-Colored Man*, their lives suggest few possibilities for improvement. Nonetheless, their search for identity is so intense and pitched that it appears, ostensibly, praiseworthy and valiant--these men strike us as Davids before a racist Goliath. But this is a phallocentric point of view. When these characters abandon/flee their families, the suggestion is that the family is barely effected because if there is a family to consider, the author spends little time developing its reaction. On the other hand, when African American women create alienated, abandoning male characters, as Toni Morrison has in the character Cholly in *The Bluest Eye*, the effects of their abandonment and flight are disturbing--especially for those abandoned. By creating a narrative voice that has a feminine point of view, readers of tales of abandonment realize a new perspective: for the women and children left behind, the results of male abandonment are as damaging as the auction block--women raise families without partners, and children grow up without the benefit of a healthy male role model. In other words, the fiction written by African American women which focuses on male abandonment illustrates a dramatic shift in point of view, emphasis, and outcome.[7]

That is why many African American women writers have depicted the theme of male flight and abandonment, not as heroic, but as demonic. In Toni Morrison's *The Bluest Eye*,[8] there are two great evils. One is Afro-America's fascination with white ideals about beauty and romance. The other is the legacy of abandonment in the African American family.

In fact, both of these themes become interwoven almost from the novel's onset, as in the scene which depicts the upcoming arrival of Mr. Henry in Claudia and Frieda's home. As Claudia listens to her mother and friends engage in the "gently wicked dance" of gossip, they overhear the reason for Mr. Henry's arrival. Mr. Henry needs a new room because the woman with whom he had been boarding, Miss Della Jones, has suffered a series of strokes. The cadre of gossiping women attribute the cause of Della Jones's strokes to her husband's abandonment of her because "'he couldn't take no more of that violet water [she] used.'" As Morrison portrays these two themes, abandonment is such an insult to the ego it leads to infirmity and craziness (Della's "'Aunt Julia is still trotting up and down Sixteenth Street talking to herself'" (p. 15)). It is further implied that Della's demise is linked to her excessive preoccupation with white ideals about beauty and hygiene: her husband "'[had] said he wanted a woman to smell like a woman. Said Della was just too clean for him'" (p. 15). In this short passage much is foretold: recurrent themes are outlined, and Morrison foreshadows the relationships of Mr. Henry/Frieda and that of Cholly/Pecola. Mr. Henry will, we learn, take advantage of his status in the home to molest Frieda. Like Cholly, Mr. Henry is a man who lives outside the bounds of propriety; as an abandoning male he is an emotional loner who preys on the innocent to assert his brand of perverse power.

Even though these men are alienated from their families at the time of their assaults, the results of their actions are not solely a measure of their depravity. They do not have that kind of power. The effect of their transgressions depends more on the integrity of the victim's self-image. It would be foolish to contend that Mr. Henry's petting of Frieda is as heinous a violation as Cholly's rape of his own daughter, Pecola. But to a large degree, I believe Morrison is suggesting that the strong egos of Frieda and Claudia, which have been fostered in a strong family environment comprised of a good mother and father, are more easily able to repel the degrading effects of Mr. Henry's perfidy:

Claudia claims "We loved him. Even after what came later, there was no bitterness in our memory of him" (p. 17). But for Pecola, her father's incest and her mother's refusal to believe her innocence in the matter, combine to shatter her fragile ego. Because her family is dysfunctional and Pecola's self-image is unsound, she shatters. Like Della Jones, who has been seduced by white values and abandoned as a result, the assault on the culturally estranged Pecola casts her into madness.

The affliction that plagues Pecola and some of the other female characters of the novel and makes them easy prey for power-frustrated males is their seduction by mass media idealizations of white beauty, idealizations which create within the Breedlove household, alienation from and shame of their blackness. As a result, both Pauline and Pecola Breedlove believe that they are ugly and worthless. Without a strong family or a sense of pride in their own cultural heritage, unable to see their way through the pervasive white value system and to keep it in perspective, these two characters learn to despise how they look and who they are. As a manifestation of her destructive fascination with the ideals of white beauty and worth, Pecola gazes "fondly at the silhouette of Shirley Temple's dimpled face" (p. 19), longing for blue eyes of her own. Mrs. Breedlove, Pecola's mother, also suffers from self-hatred; indeed, she fostered it in her own daughter.[9] For Pecola, the learning of "contempt for their own blackness" began early in life; for Pauline, it is suggested the period of conversion was longer. As it is described in the novel, Pauline's seduction by white values began when, early in her marriage, she succumbed to the popular stereotypes of beauty promulgated by white movie makers:

> ...she went to the movies.... Along with the idea of romantic love, she was introduced to another--physical beauty. Probably the most destructive ideas in the history of human thought. Both originated in envy, thrived in insecurity, and ended in disillusion....
> She was never able, after her education in the movies, to look at a face and not assign it some category in the scale of absolute beauty, and the scale was one she absorbed in full from the silver screen. (pp. 96-97)

Mrs. Breedlove's crippled foot, a symbol of her blackness, had once been a source of love between she and Cholly: "Instead of ignoring her infirmity, pretending it was not there, he made it seem like something special and endearing. For the first time Pauline felt that her bad foot was an asset" (p. 92). But as the Breedloves' relationship disintegrates, so too does Pauline's image of herself. Ultimately, Pauline, proudly though mistakenly, embraces and then defends to the exclusion of all other values, the definition bestowed upon her by the Fisher household: "the ideal servant." Both Pauline's and Pecola's egos, seduced by the barrage of mass-marketed white cliches, finally relinquish what should have been their personal, culturally grounded identities.

The tragic conversion of Pauline and Pecola Breedlove to apostles of the white creed is mirrored in Cholly's vain odyssey in search of his father and his birthright. Abandoned by both his mother and father at birth, Cholly decides to find his father after his surrogate mother, Aunt Jimmy, dies. His plans, however, are thwarted. His father doesn't recognize him, appears to have no knowledge of his existence, and refuses to acknowledge Cholly's claim on him. After his father rejects him, Cholly soils his pants "like a baby" (p. 124) and, going to a nearby river to hide, "remained knotted in [a] fetal position ... for a long time" (p. 124). Stripped of his family by death and abandonment, Cholly emerges from this episode reborn, not into a new family, but as a man without family ties and a distorted sense of propriety and responsibility. He is filled with a sense of euphoria and freedom as the chains of his past fall away. "In those days, Cholly was truly free. Abandoned in a junk heap by his mother, rejected for a crap game by his father, there was nothing more to lose. He was alone with his own perceptions and appetites, and they alone interested him" (p. 126).

Cholly's abandonment and rejection leave him without a family or culture to mold and guide him. Cholly's rebirth is thus not an initiation into society, but a regression back into self and away from community and communal values. Cholly's new found freedom then, is the freedom of estrangement, and the power he derives from it is a perversion. Like Soaphead's misanthropic conjuring, Cholly wields his brute, physical power in an attempt to create substance from nothing. Cholly and Pauline fight and argue brutally and each finds a measure of gratification and definition in those bouts: "No less did Cholly need her [Pauline]. She was one of the few things abhorrent to him that he could touch and therefore hurt. He poured out on her the sum of all his inarticulate and aborted desires. Hating her, he could leave himself intact" (p. 37). The same emotions incite Cholly to rape Pecola: "The clear statement of her misery was an accusation. He wanted to break her neck--but tenderly. Guilt and impotence rose in a bilious duet. What could he do for her--ever? What give her? What say to her? What could a burned-out black man say to the hunched back of his eleven-year-old daughter?" (p. 127). Just as, many years earlier, Cholly's powerlessness misdirected his hate at Darlene when he should have hated the white hunters who discovered the young pair making love (p. 117), so too Cholly's powerlessness in the white world and alienation and disinheritance from the black world incites him to beat Pauline and rape Pecola in attempts to assert his potency. Of course, Cholly is not potent, either literally or symbolically. Pecola's baby dies, Pecola goes mad, and Cholly, like his son Sammy, takes flight and abandons his family.

The cycle of abandonment is complete. Except that Morrison has broadened the cycle of abandonment to include more than the physical abandonment of the male; *now the process of alienation reveals that weak, culturally uprooted women psychologically abandon their African American culture and families, too.* While the reader might expect Cholly, like his father before him, to abandon the family, and then for Cholly's son Sammy, the namesake of his paternal grandfather, to also abandon the family, the more disturbing aspect of this novel is the legacy of cultural alienation (abandonment) that Pauline imparts to Pecola. Thus, Pauline teaches Pecola, by example, to love "whiteness." This conditioning places Pecola in an untenable position. Without the family support she needs to overcome her rape, and the other psychological assaults she suffers as a black child in a world teeming with white values, Pecola goes mad, just as Cholly's mother reputedly did, and just as the culturally alienated Della Jones did. In the end, Pecola's life is spent on the fringes of a dump, just as Cholly's began.

By striving to become what they cannot become, the Breedloves spread despair to their children. The story's narrator says of Pauline that: "Into her son [Sammy] she beat a loud desire to run away, and into her daughter she beat a fear of growing up, fear of other people, fear of life" (p. 102). The type of black self-hatred that Pauline embodies is not a new phenomenon. Zora Neale Hurston wondered about blacks who sang the songs of black praise out of one side of their mouths, while denigrating the blackness of blacks out of the other side:

I listened to this talk and became more and more confused. If it was so honorable and glorious to be black, why was it the yellow-skinned people among us had so much prestige? Even

a child in first grade could see this was so from what happened
in the classroom and on school programs. The light-skinned
were always the angels, fairies and queens of school plays....
Was it really honorable to be black?[10]

Hurston's observations about her own school life validate Morrison's
depiction of the demeaning treatment Pecola is subjected to at school
at the hands of students and teachers alike, solely because of the
blackness of her skin tone, especially when compared to the preferential
treatment bestowed upon the light-skinned mulatto Maureen Peal.
Hurston's comments about the perspicacity of first-graders suggests that
out of the mouths of babes shall come the truth--just as it is the
testimony of young Claudia's narrative voice that gives *The Bluest Eye*
the power to edify her readers about the evils of abandonment while at
the same time it decries the adoption of white ideals of beauty and
value in place of African American values.

Claudia's sense of true beauty is not enfeebled by Frieda'a and
Pecola's fascination with the Shirley Temple doll: "I couldn't join them
in their admiration because I hated Shirley Temple. Not because she
was cute, but because she danced with Bojangles, who was *my* friend,
my uncle, *my* daddy, and who ought to have been soft-shoeing it and
chuckling with me" (p. 19). Claudia's desires and wants are grounded
in her strong connection to her African American culture. For Christmas
she does not want a doll she "could not love"; rather, she longed for the
satisfaction of genuine emotion: "I wanted rather to feel something on
Christmas day. The real question would have been, 'Dear Claudia, what
experience would you like on Christmas?' I would have spoken up, 'I
want to sit on the low stool in Big Mama's kitchen with my lap full of
lilacs and listen to Big Papa play his violin for me alone'" (p. 21).
Claudia's ability to invent her own measures of beauty and worth,
especially in a society inundated with disingenuous models, is akin to
the powers of conjuring.

Marjorie Pryse has traced the notion of "conjuring" in the
works of black women writers and concluded that "In the 1970s and the
1980s, black women novelists have become metaphorical conjure
women,...." This history has its roots in writers preceding those two
decades, although primarily in Hurston. What these women do, Pryse
goes on to say, is to focus:

...on connection rather than separation, transforming silence into speech and giving back power to the culturally disenfranchised ...[thereby affirming] the wholeness and endurance of a vision that, once articulated, can be shared--though its heritage, roots, survival, and intimate possession belong to black women alone.[11]

Stated another way, black women writers have been able to do what modern black males writers have very often failed to do--provide models which suggest patterns and strategies for living satisfying, self-defined, culturally grounded lives. Hurston's role in this creative process was invaluable. According to Marjorie Pryse, it was Hurston who, in *Their Eyes Were Watching God,* "recreates the tradition of female friendship and shared understanding and heals the lingering impact of separation imposed by slavery and sexism."[12] And it is Toni Morrison's *The Bluest Eye,* that directly attacks two threats to the African American family and African American personal identity: the notion that abandonment of the family by black men is heroic; while also rejecting the validity of the white-is-beautiful paradigm for black women. At the same time, in the voice of an innocent narrator, Morrison allows her readers to see a successful model of self-definition as personified in the small girl, Claudia.

More than in any of her first five novels, in *The Bluest Eye,* Toni Morrison confronts the insidious capabilities of the dominant white culture in America to subsume the smaller, more fragile African American culture. When deprived of its roots and abandoned by those African Americans who perceive acculturation as a necessary means to social and economic success in American society, the African American culture and its inherent value system have been diminished and demeaned both overtly and covertly by contact with the larger white American society. Acculturation nonetheless has retained its proponents, especially in a society which professes to believe in the myth of assimilation and the American "melting pot" in which all citizens are called "Americans"--without the identifying prefix of "Afro-," "Jewish-," "Hispanic-," "Native-," etcetera.

The problem, as Morrison expresses it in this novel, is that the African American culture, despite its unique resiliency and vitality, is fighting for its life in the larger mainstream that is white American culture. If blacks succumb to the ubiquitous influence of the white American value system, then what will be left as a viable expression of the African-American culture? There are characters in *The Bluest Eye* who are pulled into the larger mainstream, blacks who fail to find the emotional and spiritual support they need from their own culture--either through bad example, or because they have no example--and so, abandon their heritage and doom themselves and their families to lives of isolation and alienation. As Trudier Harris has stated in her recent work, *Fiction and Folklore: The Novels of Toni Morrison*:

> Though Claudia's family provides an oasis in the desert of mythological infertility in the novel, Morrison's world is primarily one in which stagnation is the norm, and where the pursuit of values alien to one's culture ultimately leads to destruction. The seasons of infertility become a metaphor for a larger condition that wears away at the very foundation of the society.[13]

The Breedloves, of course, represent a family of alienation, infertility, and stagnation. But the Breedloves are not alone in this failure and *The Bluest Eye* is not simply the tale of Pecola Breedlove and her madness. Nor is the novel the tale of one little girl who believes she is ugly and hopes for acceptance through the beautifying power of eyes that are bluer than Shirley Temple's.

    The Bluest Eye is not a chronologically told tale; the reader knows from the onset of the novel about Pecola's rape and the deaths of Pecola's baby and of Cholly. Nearly as soon, the reader knows that Cholly has put his family "outdoors"--the worst thing, Claudia confides, a man could do to his family. As a result, *The Bluest Eye* is not so much about fallen people as it about the processes that cause the fall; it is not so much about forcible rape as it is about the forces that corrupt. *The Bluest Eye* is the tale of African American families who both succeed and fail in the successful transmission of meaningful and supportive cultural values to their offspring. It is the tale of those families who succumb to the allure of the dominant white cultural mainstream as epitomized in the trope "blue eyes," and those families who discover value in their own African American culture as expressed, most succinctly, in the philosophy of "the blues." Quite rightly, Trudier

Harris has claimed that: "Claudia's recounting of Pecola's tragedy is in
the tradition of blues narrative."[14] Morrison, as she would do in her later
novels, explores the vitality of the African-American culture within her
novel by juxtaposing characters and families who represent the
culturally grounded and the culturally uprooted.[15] Claudia, Frieda, and
their parents, clearly represent the "grounded" characters in *The Bluest
Eye*, and the ironically named Breedloves,[16] among others, represent the
"uprooted." Enveloping this framework are the larger oppositional forces
of the African-American and the white Western cultures. When Claudia
begins her narrative in the first section of the novel, "Autumn," the very
first images she presents to the reader resonate with the power and
pervasiveness of Western culture as background to the novel. Claudia
states:

> Nuns go by as quiet as lust, the drunken men and sober eyes
> sing in the lobby of the Greek hotel. Rosemary Villanucci, our
> next-door friend who lives above her father's cafe, sits in a
> 1939 Buick eating bread and butter. She rolls down the
> window to tell my sister Frieda and me that we can't come in.
> We stare at her, wanting the bread, but more than that wanting
> to poke the arrogance out of her eyes and smash the pride of
> ownership that curls her chewing mouth. (p. 12)

Nuns, a Greek hotel, a girl with an Italian name: together the images of
this scene suggest Catholicism, Christian thought and tradition, and the
two cradles of ancient Western civilization--Greece and Rome; and in
the picture of the traditionally garbed "nuns," the racial conflicts of
black and white are immediately presented. These are the forces, the
"breads" of the larger white society which Claudia knows and can see,
but which are denied to her as a black girl: "She [Rosemary Villanucci]
rolls down the window to tell my sister Frieda and me that we can't
come in." It is these icons she wishes to smash, but cannot, unless
reduced to the stature of a doll with blue eyes.

    As a narrator, Claudia's voice is strong and certain; she knows
Pecola's life is tragic, and she presents enough of her own family life
to illustrate where her own strengths and where Pecola's weaknesses
come from. Like much of James Baldwin's *Go Tell It on the Mountain*,
The Bluest Eye is told in retrospect, focusing on the past histories of the
principle adult characters. And justly so, for it is the adult characters

who are the purveyors of their culture and their lives and experiences impact on the lives of their children. Equally, Morrison also relies heavily on the signification of character traits to define the roles of the novel's principles. As a result, the reader while learning precious little about Claudia's parents, recognizes that when Mrs. Mac Teer is portrayed as singing the blues--"She would sing about hard times, bad times, and somebody-done-gone-and-left-me times" (p. 24)--that she is "culturally grounded," despite the fact that she talks down to her daughter on occasion and mindlessly gives her daughters blue-eyed dolls at Christmas time. Precious little is said about Claudia's father, either. But he responds to Mr. Henry's molestation of Frieda so forcefully, the reader recognizes a solid family structure with strong moral values. In such an environment, it's not surprising Claudia has her head on straight, even if she willfully decapitates her blue-eyed dolls.

Of the minor characters in *The Bluest Eye* little more need be said or inferred. Signifying language is sufficient, just as it is in an early scene of James Baldwin's *Go Tell It on the Mountain*, in which John Grimes is portrayed in language that aligns him to High John the Conqueror, the mythic trickster of African American folklore who is so powerful that he can defeat the Devil.[17] Characterizing John in such mythic terms clearly foreshadows *and validates* his religious conversion and inclusion in the community at the novel's conclusion. A conversion which, not insignificantly, would lose much of its dramatic power if the personal (i.e., cultural) histories of his elders were not the major focus of the novel. Morrison's novel mimics this strategy.

Morrison sketches many of her characters via signification. Claudia's parents are culturally grounded and impart that rootedness to their daughters. Conversely, both Maureen Peal, a mulatto girl adored because of the lightness of her skin, and Geraldine,[18] who possesses social pretensions and sexual frigidity, are easily classified in the culturally uprooted group because of their feelings of superiority, especially as a result of their shameful behavior when dealing with Pecola. Soaphead Church's name implies that white soap bubbles have whitewashed his mind and, more obliquely, aligns him with Christianity, a religion alien to Africa-American humanism. Pauline and Cholly Breedlove, who will be discussed at more length shortly, are also portrayed in a manner which clearly defines their groundedness, or lack of it. All of these characters are not so much developed in the novel as they are signified, or revealed as types.

By opting to portray characters by signifying, and at the same time downplay character development, Morrison suggests an element of determinism in *The Bluest Eye.* Morrison creates a world in which strong, proud families are able to impart their ideals and a sense of identity to their children; while weak families fall prey to society's more pernicious and ineffectual fallacies--as if subject to forces beyond their control. Morrison would move away from determinism in her later novels by reducing the overt importance of white culture upon her characters, as has been suggested by Cynthia Davis already in this chapter; but certainly in *The Bluest Eye* these social forces play a role.

Pecola's story is tragic not because of a flaw in her personality (or her lack of stature), but because of a flaw in her family and its sense of heritage and identity. Pecola's fate is not really "personal," but emblematic and characteristic of the fate of many African-Americans. It is the portraits of Pecola's parents, Pauline (Williams) and Cholly Breedlove, which are most important to the novel. Clearly, Morrison meant to contrast the youths of Cholly and Pauline to suggest how their respective families influenced the development of their personalities.

It is in the section labelled "Spring," that the tales of Cholly's and Pauline's youth are told. The section's title is heavily ironic, for it contains five different stories, each of which results not in growth, but in a grotesque and perverse rite of initiation/passage. Frieda is molested by Mr. Henry. Pauline is "seduced" by the white value system inherent in the Fisher household and is "transformed" into Polly, the perfect maid; earlier in her life, Pauline is seduced by images of white beauty as portrayed on the silver screen. Cholly's first sexual encounter becomes a source of shame and humiliation to him as a result of two white hunters who discover him in the act and shine a flashlight on him making a "moon of his behind" (p. 117). Pecola is raped by her father, Cholly. And finally, we learn about Soaphead Church's molestation of young girls and of his ego-maniacal deceit of Pecola.

"Spring" is full of vivid details, especially about Cholly and Pauline, and goes far to explain how the forces of the dominant white cultural can overwhelm and corrupt a less vital African American culture. Pauline's youth is sketched crudely by Morrison, as she relies on signifiers to outline her character--which is broadly illustrated as a collection of weaknesses. One of nine children, "she alone of all the children had no nickname" (p. 88). She is also described, more than once, as liking "to arrange things" (p. 88), to make order out of things.

As benign as these two character traits appear to the larger white culture, within the African-American community these traits displace Pauline and make her feel separate and unworthy (p. 88)--although she blames that on her foot, a condition over which she has no control. In a culture in which "naming" has significant implications, Pauline's lack of a nickname leaves her, symbolically, without any identity to bind her to her family, especially when nicknames are bestowed as a result of memorable events or personality traits. Pauline's need for order suggests a lack of spontaneity in her personality, an inability to improvise. This trait explains why she is unable to be happy when early in her marriage Cholly was away at work and she was left alone in her apartment to herself. She needed him to provide stability, meaning, and order in her life. We are also told about Pauline that "she was enchanted by numbers and depressed by words" (p. 89). As a member of an essentially oral culture, a blues-based culture which values verbal improvisation, Pauline is out of touch with her heritage and, therefore, easily seduced by a white culture in which logic, order, and structure are highly valued. Because her family finds nothing notable about her and because Cholly is not willing to support her clinginess, Pauline turns to white society for acceptance, identity, and self-esteem, all of which she gains. But, the novel asks implicitly, at what cost to herself? And, consequently, at what cost to her family, especially Pecola?

Cholly's life is less easy to pigeon-hole. Abandoned by both his mother and father as a baby, Cholly might easily have lost his sense of identity, as Pauline did. But Cholly is given a second chance when he is rescued and raised by his Aunt Jimmy, and befriended by Blue Jack. Within this nurturing community, Cholly is given self-esteem, a knowledge of his folk culture, and a sense of his race's history in America. From Blue Jack, Cholly also acquires a blues sensibility. About Blue Jack we are told that when he spoke: "His voice was both sad and pleased" (p. 107). Blue Jack's name and the ambiguous tonal qualities of his voice clearly signify that he is a "blues" character. Exposed to the blues through his friendship with Blue Jack, Cholly assumes their outlook naturally; thus when Pauline and Cholly met, Cholly was whistling a blues-inspired tune: "a kind of city-street music where laughter belies anxiety, and joy is as short and straight as the blade of a pocket knife" (p. 91). To further delineate Cholly's blues personality, we also learn (after Cholly's unsuccessful attempt to claim his father and his rebirth in the river) that:

Only a musician would sense, know, without even knowing
that he knew, that Cholly was free. Dangerously free. Free to
feel whatever he felt--fear, guilt, shame, love, grief, pity. Free
to be tender or violent, to whistle or weep.... In those days,
Cholly was truly free.... He was alone with his own
perceptions and appetites, and they alone interested him. (pp.
125-26)[19]

By this point in the novel all of the major characters have been
described, except Soaphead Church, whose life-story is later sketched,
in the same manner that Pauline's was, with the end result of making
him a cultural outsider, a member of the "blue eyes" set.

Cholly, however, presents a problem. He is clearly a "blues"
character. As such, while we recognize that he is a bearer of his race's
culture and traditions, and thus an insider, he is also, because of his
rape of Pecola, an outsider, a point Claudia is clear to establish (pp. 17-
19). Even Morrison's description of Cholly's rape is laced with
ambivalent language: "Surrounding all of his lust was a border of
politeness. He wanted to fuck her--tenderly" (p. 128). But just as the
trickster's role in African-American lore is often ambivalent, so too does
ambivalence signify the emotional posture of the blues man.

The most significant problem of interpretation in the novel
arises in an evaluation of Cholly. Because he is both an outsider, as a
result of his abandonment and putting his family "outside," and because
he is also a cultural insider, as a blues man who purveys certain African
American culture values, his character is a problematic, fusion of
opposites. The problem is compounded when we consider that
elsewhere in the novel, when Morrison has utilized the blues to define
a character's groundedness in the African American culture, that usage
has been clear cut. In Mrs. Mac Teer's singing of the blues and in
Claudia's attraction to them (pp. 24, 78), in Blue Jack (p. 107), in the
combined voices of Aunt Jimmy, Miss Alice, and Mrs. Gaines as they
spoke together before Aunt Jimmy dies on peach cobbler (pp. 109-10)--
in all of these instances, the "blues" signify that these characters are
grounded in their culture. An affinity for the blues validates and
solidifies these characters' positions in the novel as purveyors of their
heritage and culture and justifies the reader's positive feeling for Mrs.
Mac Teer, Claudia, Blue Jack, and the three women whose voices meld
as one. In these characters, their blues outlook is a certain signifier of

their rootedness to their culture. In this group of blues-based characters, Morrison has avoided ambivalence in their characterization.

Other characters are also linked to the blues in some fashion. The hooker Poland is one such character; however, she plays such a minor role in the novel that her predilection for the blues (despite the double-irony of her name: a culture-based nickname, that sounds ethnically Western) is of little consequence other than explaining the three hookers' mutual affinity for and tolerance of Pecola. In an ingenious inversion, Soaphead Church is described in such blatantly anti-blues language that the vocabulary of blues, in his case, serves to clearly cast him outside of his African American heritage. Morrison writes of Soaphead: "Living there among his worn things, rising early every morning from dreamless sleeps, he counseled those who sought his advice. His business was dread. People came to him in dread, whispered in dread, wept and pleaded in dread. And dread was what he counseled" (p. 136). In Soaphead's counsel there is nothing to suggest a blues outlook, no desire to find a balance to life's difficulties, no positive affirmation is sought to overcome the "dread." Soaphead is clearly a demonic character in the novel whose sense of pride and racial superiority allow him to treat those he considers his inferiors with contempt.

It is in the face of these more clear-cut blues characterizations that the interpretation of Cholly's character presents a difficulty. As discussed earlier, Cholly is guilty of abandonment and of passing on that legacy to his son, Sammy, thereby meriting the reader's censure. Cholly's pitiful rape of Pecola is also a despicable act, to say the least. Yet for all of that, Cholly's past, which is described in more detail than any other character's, has a mitigating effect on the reader's judgment of him. It would be unfair to neglect or negate the acculturation process detailed in Morrison's description of Cholly's youth, especially when Morrison meant for Pauline's and Cholly's pasts to be clear indicators of their cultural (un)groundedness. Why else would Morrison tie Cholly to the blues legacy, which is positively portrayed, if not to soften and ameliorate the reader's censure of Cholly's raping of his own daughter when, blues artist or not, most readers would be hard pressed to discover something positive in Cholly's raping of his daughter?

In his essay, "Roadblocks and Relatives: Critical Revision in Toni Morrison's *The Bluest Eye*," Michael Awkward has argued that Morrison modeled Cholly's rape of Pecola on Trueblood's rape of his daughter in Ralph Ellison's *Invisible Man*. Awkward also argues that Claudia's dismemberment of her dolls is patterned after Bigger Thomas's dismemberment of Mary Dalton in Richard Wright's *Native Son*. His arguments, based on these works' intertextuality, are clear, persuasive, and responsible. What Awkward suggests finally is that Morrison has, in *The Bluest Eye*, forced a reversal of the phallocentric reading of these novels as espoused by such notable critics as Houston Baker in his *Blues, Ideology, and Afro-American Literature,* by focusing on the fate of the victim of the rape and not on the male assailants. Awkward states:

> Morrison finally seems to be taking Ellison to task for the phallocentric nature of his representations of incest that marginalizes and renders as irrelevant the consequences of the act for the female victim. Morrison writes her way into the Afro-American literary tradition by bringing to the foreground the effects of incest for female victims in direct response to Ellison's refusal to consider them seriously. So while the victims of incest in both novels ultimately occupy similarly asocial, silent positions in their respective communities, Morrison explicitly details Pecola's tragic and painful journey, while Ellison, in confining Matty Lou to the periphery, suggest that her perspective contains for him "no compelling significance."[20]

Awkward's point is well taken. But while he has insightfully delineated some of *The Bluest Eye's* antecedents, I do not agree with him that the novel is about Pecola. Rather, the novel is about the process of cultural erosion that effects the novel's characters. Pecola's descent into madness is too lengthy a process and the result of too many influences to be reduced, finally, to a single moment's outcome. Pecola doesn't go crazy because of the rape, but because her ego is too small and fragile to sustain the injury--*and because she gets no support from her mother*.

Rather than being a novel about Pecola, I believe *The Bluest Eye* is about Claudia and Pauline, especially Pauline. (Claudia's role is to be a critical narrator, intimate and judgmental after years of contemplation.) It is, I believe, ultimately Pauline's seduction by ideals of white beauty that are responsible for the devastating effects of Cholly's rape on Pecola. Pauline does not support Pecola after the rape;

and it is the insidious effects of Pauline's belittled ego that force the deterioration of Cholly's blues sensibilities, corrupting and weakening them to the point that he is capable of committing his crime against his family and his daughter. As a result, the Cholly who rapes at the novel's end is little like the Cholly who lived with Aunt Jimmy and was friends with Blue Jack. He too has been demeaned and perverted by prolonged contact with Pauline.

I feel Morrison aligned Cholly with the blues deliberately to ensure that judgment and censure of him was ameliorated. Without his blues connections, readers would condemn Cholly wholeheartedly and feel certain that it was his rape that caused Pecola's madness. Cause and effect would appear clear cut. But because Morrison has worked to soften our feelings for Cholly by aligning him with the blues, readers are urged to look elsewhere for blame. And clearly the blame--not for the rape itself, but for the *process* that led up to the rape--is Pauline's. Cholly may have raped Pecola, but the description of the incident implies Cholly loved Pecola--even if perversely and wrongly, even if his affections were in response to latent feelings for Pauline as he first knew her when he was still young and free. If any act of abuse most merits the reader's condemnation, it is not Cholly's rape of Pecola, but Pauline's rejection of her own child in favor of the white Fisher child. This scene more than any other exemplifies Pauline's disgust with her family and blackness. Outraged at Pecola's clumsiness for spilling "blackish blueberries" all over the Fisher's clean floor, Claudia narrates that Pauline hit Pecola "with the back of her hand [and] knocked her to the floor.... yanked her up by the arm, slapped her again." As Claudia describes the scene's ending, an angry Pauline "spit out words to us like rotten apples" (p. 87). In a kitchen of "white porcelain [and] white woodwork," the spilt *blackish* blueberries are an affront to the whiteness Pauline has worked so hard to maintain. If Pauline has found her Eden in the Fisher home, then Claudia rightly understands that Pauline's apple-words are as rotten as is her understanding of good and evil. It is Pauline who has sinned against herself and her family by abandoning them for a false cultural models and it is her sin which casts Pecola into darkness and a legacy of shame and madness.

Lawrence W. Levine has claimed in his *Black Culture and Black Consciousness* that: "It is hardly surprising that the deeply ingrained prejudices of American society should have affected some of its victims to the point where they turned the hatred upon themselves and their peers."[21] The process of creating a self-hatred so strong that it can destroy those around oneself is the central tale of *The Bluest Eye*.

If Morrison has accomplished something noteworthy in *The Bluest Eye*, it is that she has redrawn the importance of women in the family, especially if male protagonists are going to abandon their families. It is the women left behind who must maintain the cultural identity of their race. Of course, if black women are seduced by false cultural models and values, then they too pose a threat to the cultural integrity of their children and their culture. *The Bluest Eye* presents a strong argument that if it is to be the role of women to guard the self-image and destiny of today's African-American family, then all black women need to recognize the forces that threaten their integrity, both from without and within.

NOTES

1. Deborah Gray White, "The Nature of Female Slavery," *Women's America: Reforming the Past*, ed. Linda K. Kerber and Jane DeHart-Mathews (New York: Oxford University Press, 1987), pp. 100-14.

2. Cynthia A. Davis, "Self, Society, And Myth in Toni Morrison's Fiction," *Contemporary Literature* 23, no. 3 (summer 1982): p. 341.

3. Richard Wright, *Native Son* (New York: Harper & Row, 1987), pp. 13-14.

4. Houston Baker discusses the character of such (abandoning) males in *Blues, Ideology*. Focusing on Richard Wright's black boy, Baker outlines a ritualistic pattern that recognizes, first, that all African Americans face a "'life-crisis' of black identity" in any "white-dominated society." This crisis is instituted by the black's awareness that in a white society, blacks represent a "zero image." As a result, black narratives are a fictive representation of passage rites which have three steps: 1) "the black person's separation from a dominant, white society"; 2) "a renewal of desire"; 3) "aggregation." These rites render "reintegration into a 'white' society impossible.... What is possible is *entry* into the singularity at the black (W)hole's center." In this sense, black flight from white society, racism, and oppression is an artist (as language and literature) exploration of what it means to be black in America , and thus is a (re)writing/righting of the black experience and black identity. Seen in that light, Baker presents an argument supporting such narrative "rites" as part of the African American culture's efforts at self-definition in a white society. However, my point remains: when the male characters of these fictive works, as characters, do not or cannot return to their families after taking flight, their "rites" still harm those left behind. (*Blues, Ideology, and Afro-American Literature* [Chicago: University of Chicago Press, 1984], pp. 152-54.)

Henry Louis Gates has written of Wright's black boy that: "Wright's humanity is achieved only at the expense of his fellow blacks....", a point which more supports my perspective. (*The Signifying Monkey* [New York: Oxford University Press, 1988], p.182.)

Certainly, as works of art, these fictions accomplish more than their characters do--but that is a point not at issue here.

5. Cynthia Davis, Ibid., p. 335.

6. Ibid., p. 335.

7. In addition to Morrison's *The Bluest Eye*, I am referring *Sula*, in which Eva's husband BoyBoy, Nel's husband Jude, and Sula's lover Ajax all of whom leave their women. I refer also to Gloria Naylor's *The Women of Brewster Street*, especially the lives of Mattie Michael, who after a lifetime of toil, is economically ruined when her son jumps bond and takes flight, and Lucielia Louise Turner, who has an abortion at her husband's insistence, then is abandoned by her husband. Coincidentally, when "Ceil's" husband leaves, Ceil's daughter is electrocuted and dies. I am also thinking of Alice Walker's short story, "The Revenge of Hannah Kemhuff," in which Hannah's husband abandons the family during the depression resulting in the death of Hannah's children and Hannah's turn to prostitution. Other examples exist as well.

8. *The Bluest Eye* (New York: Washington Square Press, 1972). All references to this novel are to this edition and are denoted by number in parentheses.

9. The description of Pauline's attempt to dominate and subjugate Pecola's will foreshadows Helene Wright's attempts to mold Nel in *Sula*.

10. *Dust Tracks on a Road: An Autobiography*, Second Edition (Urbana: University of Illinois Press, 1984), p. 226.

11. "Zora Neale Hurston, Alice Walker, and the 'Ancient Power' of Black Women," *Conjuring: Black Women, Fiction, and Literary Tradition*, ed. Marjorie Pryse and Hortense J. Spillers (Bloomington: Indiana University Press, 1985), p. 5.

12. Ibid., p. 15.

13. *Fiction and Folklore: The Novels of Toni Morrison* (Knoxville: University of Tennessee Press, 1991), p. 28.

The insidious nature of the larger white culture's ability to corrupt the idealization of beauty, of both the weak and the strong, is also the theme of Ann Petry's short story, "Mother Africa." In that story a black junk man, who is a drop-out, comes to own a statue he calls Mother Africa. Feeling she is black, the beauty of the statue works a curious effect on him. He cleans his yard, plants grass around her, making a small park because of the statue. Then finally he is driven to cut his hair and beard after twenty-five years. But then when taking a cheap dress off of the statue, he discovers, much to his surprise, that the figure has white facial features and so he scraps it.

14. *Fiction and Folklore*, Ibid., p. 26.

15. The concepts of the culturally grounded and the culturally uprooted is more thoroughly discussed in the follow chapter on the novel *Sula*.

16. Pecola's name also appears to be highly ironic. Zora Neale Hurston has defined the word "Pe-ola" as: "a very white Negro girl"; see *Spunk: The Selected Stories*, (Berkeley, CA: Turtle Island Foundation, 1985), p. 94.

17. *Go Tell It on the Mountain* (New York: Signet Books, 1963), pp. 30-31.

18. Geraldine bears a remarkable resemblance to a future character of Morrison's: Helene Wright of *Sula*.

19. Cholly as a blues man certainly suggests the blues character Sula in Morrison's second novel, *Sula*. Both characterizations are marked by ambiguity, both for readers and fellow characters in their respective novels.

20. "Roadblocks and Relatives: Critical Revision in Toni Morrison's *The Bluest Eye*," *Critical Essays on Toni Morrison*, ed. Nellie Y. McKay (Boston: G.K. Hall & Co., 1988), p. 66.

21. *Black Culture and Black Consciousness: Afro-American Thought From Slavery To Freedom* (New York: Oxford University Press, 1977), p. 285.

V

THE BLUES IN *SULA*

The novels and narratives examined so far have argued that the
development of strong family bonds and community ties are essential
to the health of the individual ego. It is important to keep in mind,
however, that within the African American family, maintaining such
bonds was not always an option. Nor, as the womanist prose of Alice
Walker contends, are all of the culturally defined roles for individuals
always in the best interest of the individual. Communities and
societies, once established, seem determined to maintain their
integrity and authority, even at the cost of the single individual.

In her second novel, *Sula*[1] (1973), Toni Morrison turns the
tables on this equation by presenting the apocalyptic demise of a small
African American community, the Bottom, after the death of its central
character, Sula. It will be the argument of this chapter that Sula's death,
at first welcomed by the Bottom, results ultimately in its demise. That
the death of a single individual could create such ruin in a community
is not the result of Sula's character alone, nor could it be; rather, the
effect of Sula's death has such magnitude because of what she
represents. In a series of arguments, I will show that Sula is a blues
character and that her character signifies the blues. As a blues trope,
Sula represents the vitality of her folk community. When the Bottom
becomes dislocated from its cultural heritage as expressed in the blues,
the Bottom and its inhabitants are swept into oblivion.

To discuss Sula as a trope, or as a signifier of the blues
requires an understanding of the nature of signifying. In the introduction
to this work, I offered a brief summary of Henry Louis Gates'
discussion of signifying as presented in *The Signifying Monkey*.[2]

Because there are a number of salient points about signifying which are germane to this chapter, I shall briefly outline some of Gates' other points here. The first is that signifying is a means of communication, using spoken and/or body language (p. 69), and it involves an element of indirection (p. 80). As Gates says: "All definitions of Signifyin(g) that do not distinguish between manner and matter succumb ... to serious misreading" (p.70). Furthermore: "Signifyin(g) is the black trope of all other tropes, the trope of tropes, the figure of figures. Signifyin(g) is troping" (p. 81). It is also Gates' estimation that "Signifyin(g) alone serves to underscore the uniqueness of the black community's use of language" (p. 81). Foremost, Signifyin(g) is "the figurative difference between the literal and the metaphorical, between surface and latent meaning" (p. 82). It should also be noted that signifying also includes the literary discourse of intertextuality, in which later writers either alter or deviate from earlier works, thereby signifying upon them. What I am proposing is that the character Sula is a signifier, is a trope, is much more than a character in a novel. The language of the novel, the folk tale idiom it utilizes, and the emphasis on improvisational skills all combine to suggest that the Bottom is a mythic place. It is a blues space, grown out of broken promises and economic suffering, heart-break and loss. In this environment, Sula is an avatar of the blues, a numinous signifier of the African American experience. Sula is the blues.

Sula is not aligned to the blues by Morrison overtly--she is not a blues singer, for instance. What establishes Sula as a blues figure is first and foremost her *improvisational nature*. To illustrate the magnitude of Sula's role as a signifier of the blues and the importance of the blues philosophy to the Bottom and, by extension, the entire African American community, I will focus on these major issues: 1. The critical arguments which contend that Sula is "evil," and suggest a broader reading; 2. The role of improvisation in defining the blues and Sula's improvisational nature; 3. Morrison's portrayal of the Bottom as folk based and thus a rich soil in which folk culture, heritage, and the blues should grow, yet ultimately perish; 4. The cultural uprootedness and groundedness of the Wright and Peace households; 5. Sula's role as a paradigm of the blues and why that is essential to the vitality of the Bottom.

Perhaps the most perplexing difficulty in assessing Toni Morrison's novel is the reader's evaluation of the title character. Is Sula evil? Is Sula good? If Sula is evil, why is she so often called heroic by critics; and why do readers find her appealing despite her faults? Toni Morrison herself commented in a 1977 interview that in creating the character Sula, it was her intention to present "...a woman who could be used as a *classic type of evil force*"[3] (emphasis added). But Morrison's intentions were not so simplistic. In the same interview, Morrison elaborated upon her plans for the novel's two central characters, Sula and Nel.

> Sula was hard, for me; very difficult to make up that kind of character. Not difficult to think up, but difficult to describe a woman who could be used as a classic type of evil force.... And at the same time, I didn't want to make her freakish or repulsive or unattractive. I was interested at that time in doing a very old, worn-out idea, which was to do something with good and evil, but putting it in different terms. And I wanted Nel to be a warm, conventional woman, one of those people you know are going to pay the gas bill and take care of the children.... And they are magnificent....[4]

Alternating currents of attraction and repulsion are what make Sula an intriguing character. But despite Morrison's stated intentions, few critics are willing to call Sula unequivocally evil. In the same 1977 interview, Morrison softened her own judgement of Sula, adding that "she [Sula] never does anything as bad as her grandmother did."[5] Melvin Dixon has said that, "'Dangerous' more than evil is an accurate description of Sula."[6] Cynthia Davis has labeled Sula a scapegoat.[7] In an essay which traces black female characters in the novels *Jubilee, Their Eyes Were Watching God,* and *Sula,* Hortense J. Spillers has praised Morrison and her ability to create in Sula "a literal and figurative *breakthrough* toward the assertion of what we may call, in relation to the her literary 'relatives,' a new female being."[8] Spillers later summarized the character of Sula:

> Sula is both loved and hated by the reader, embraced and rejected simultaneously because her audience is forced to accept the corruption of absolutes and what has been left in their place--the complex, alienated, transitory gestures of a

personality who has no framework of moral reference beyond
or other than herself.[9]

If anything about the character of Sula warrants the label of
"evil," it may be her role as an outsider. Given the temperament of the
Bottom in the 1930s, Sula could be criticized for her selfishness and
detachment; any ascribing of evil to Sula may spring from these
attempts at self-definition as well as an emphasis on her dark blues side,
what Houston Baker has referred to as the "black blues life."[10] Hortense
Spillers suggests that: "... Sula is woman-for-self," and that result of
such self(ish)ness is that: "In Sula's case, the old love of the collective,
for the collective, is lost, and passions are turned antagonistic...."[11] Seen
in this light, Sula appears to be the female incarnation of the blues
character Cholly Breedlove for the novel *The Bluest Eye.*

Because the citizens of the Bottom still cling to traditional
values, Sula attracts their criticism for rejecting the expectation that she
associate with and accept definition from the larger community, as Nel
does. In a very real way, Sula refuses to accept a traditional role within
the "pre-individual" group of the Bottom.[12] As Ralph Ellison has
described the concept, the pre-individual group is a means for the black
community to coalesce and, by stressing, indeed demanding, uniformity
of action in the face of white oppression and racism, for the group to
maintain its integrity and safety. As Ellison explains, Wright's black
boy, in rejecting the notion of the pre-individual by asserting his own
individuality, threatens the entire group's safety and, as a result, the
group retaliates by repeatedly punishing the youth physically. The
example of Wright's black boy is easily superimposed on Sula. She too
refuses to be defined as an anonymous member of the group and rebels
against conformity, and with similar outcome: she is ostracized and
despised as a threat to the integrity of the Bottom. Houston Baker, in
his *Long Black Song*, reiterates Wright's sense of the importance of the
collective ethos in African American culture:

...black American culture was never characterized by the
individual ethos of white American culture.... Black American
culture is characterized by the collectivistic ethos; society is
not viewed as a protective arena in which the individual can
work out his own destiny and gain a share of America's

benefits by his own efforts. To the black American these
benefits are not attained solely by the individual effort....[13]

As an "outsider" and a threat, Sula is associated with the
plague of robins by the members of the Bottom; to the reader, Sula
appears threatening because of her role in Chicken Little's death and for
her failure to act when witnessing her mother, Hannah, burn to death.
By further rejecting the prescribed roles of wife and mother, and by
betraying her responsibility to her grandmother Eva, Sula seems to
deserve the label "evil." Yet, this is not reason enough to condemn Sula,
not when, for most readers, Sula's assertion of self and her efforts at
self-definition appear heroic. Contemporary readers can certainly recall
the praise showered on Alice Walker's character Celie in *The Color
Purple* (1982) for finally rejecting her "God-given" roles in that novel.
But unlike Celie's personal development in *The Color Purple*, Sula's
heroism is not accurately a result of growing feminism; nor is it a result
of increasing self-awareness. In Walker's novel, Celie grows in self-
awareness, esteem, and assertiveness, and her growth is reflected in
those around her. Nothing of that magnitude occurs in *Sula*; Sula's
heroism is not the result of feminist tendencies or awareness. *Rather,
the heroic qualities Sula embodies comes from the fact that in this
lyrical novel, Sula signifies the blues, is a numinous incarnation of her
blues cultural heritage.* It is Sula-as-blues and the vibrant expression of
folk experience which she embodies which are the subject of this novel
and which make Sula heroic.

In his introduction to *Blues, Ideology, and Afro-American
Literature*, Houston Baker states that:

> The guiding presupposition of [*Blues, Ideology*] is that Afro-
> American culture is a complex, reflexive enterprise which finds
> its proper figuration in blues conceived as a matrix. A matrix
> is a womb, a network.... A matrix is a point of ceaseless input
> and output, crisscrossing impulses always in productive transit.
> Afro-American blues constitute such a vibrant network.... They
> are the multiplex, enabling *script* in which Afro-American
> cultural discourse is inscribed.[14]

The major energies and force of Baker's work is to work out and
display, and at times to rewrite, an approach to African American

literature which utilizes the *vernacular of the blues* as a starting point
when interpreting African American literature critically, as this chapter
will do. Using his theory of a *blues matrix* as a critical springboard,
Baker illustrates how the modern critic can discover new meaning and
significance in such long forgotten and disregarded works as Paul
Laurence Dunbar's *The Sport of the Gods* (1901), for instance.

Dunbar's novel tells the story of the mistaken and tragic
indictment of an innocent black man for a robbery he did not commit.
What is most significant to Baker's treatise, and to this particular
chapter, is that it takes a character Baker describes as a "blues
detective" to uncover the truth, to right the wrong. This blues detective
is a yellow journalist from the north, a Mr. Skaggs. Baker says of
Skaggs that, "One might equate such a creatively *improvisational hero*
with the *bricoleur*, or handyman, who assesses a problem and employs
tools at hand to achieve nonce solutions. What is crucial to the work of
the blues detective is his ability to break away from traditional concepts
and to supply new and creative possibilities" (first emphasis added).
Baker goes on to claim that, "Only sharp, *improvisationally* creative
skills can ensure his success. And the slapdash creativity of his
enterprise--the rough-and-ready, 'jamming' motion that carries him
toward some newly expressive work--makes him equivalent to the artist
seeking to bring forth some 'nontraditional' product"[15] (emphasis added).

It is the *improvisational skills* of the blues detective Skaggs
that Baker admires about Dunbar's novel, *The Sport of the Gods*; as it
is the improvisational skills of the artist that constitute a central part of
the blues matrix because improvisation is an essential component of the
blues. It has been claimed that the greatness of pianist Art Tatum's blues
artistry was his improvisational skills. Improvisation was also one of the
most lauded skills of Louis Armstrong. It is the argument of this chapter
that the character Sula is part of the blues matrix Baker so carefully
delineates in *Blues, Ideology*. The tone of the novel suggests that Sula
is more than a one-dimensional character. She is improvisational--that
is the most important thing.[16] She is also artistic and individualistic--and
that is the problematic thing. She is also a paradigm of the blues, and
Morrison frequently describes Sula in terms that define the
blues.

What are the blues, and how do the blues specifically relate to Sula the character and *Sula* the novel? Perhaps the most acclaimed definition of the blues was written by Ralph Ellison:

> The blues is an impulse to keep the painful details and episodes of a brutal experience alive in one's aching consciousness, to finger its jagged grain, and to transcend it, not by the consolation of philosophy but by squeezing from it a near-tragic, near-comic lyricism. As a form, the blues is an autobiographical chronicle of personal catastrophe expressed lyrically.[17]

Ellison's eloquent definition smoothly fits Sula as character and as novel. If the reader of *Sula* will consider the novel as a blues song and the character Sula as a signifier of the blues, Sula's seemingly cold and callous role in the death of Chicken Little and her equally disturbing inaction while observing the death of her mother, assume a different dimension. If Sula were the same as the other characters in the novel, she might deserve our condemnation as evil for her role in those two deaths. But if Sula is viewed as blues statement, and as an expression of life's "brutal experience," an expression which the people of the Bottom can use to judge and evaluate their own experiences and values--as so often happens in the novel--then Sula's role assumes another, more metaphorical, level of meaning. Indeed, the novel says of Sula, "she simply helped others define themselves" (p. 95). As blues expression, her role of forcing others to define themselves becomes existential--that is, by forcing the members of the Bottom to define what they believe and what mores they uphold, those members move from mere existence to essence, to use Sartre's definition of being.[18]

Certain critical evaluations of Sula's character can be resolved if Sula is viewed as a signifier of the blues. For instance, Hortense Spillers has claimed: "Insofar as Sula is not a loving human being, extending few of the traditional loyalties to those around her, she reverses the customary trend of 'moral growth' and embodies, contrarily, a figure of genuine moral ambiguity about whom few comforting conclusions may be drawn."[19] To consider Sula as "blues" goes far to explain the ambiguity associated with an assessment of Sula's character. In fact, according to Leroi Jones, the blues contain a number of tensions, not the least of which are the tensions between the African and

American cultures and, respectively, their collectivistic and individualistic ethos. Jones says:

> ...African songs dealt,... with the exploits of the social unit, usually the tribe.... but the insistence of blues verse on the life of the individual and his individual trials and successes on the earth is a manifestation of the whole Western concept of man's life, and it is a development that could only be found in an American black man's music.... The whole concept of the *solo*, of a man singing or playing by himself, was relatively unknown in West African music.
>   ...blues ... went back for its impetus and emotional meaning to the individual, to his completely personal life and death.[20]

Sula is the individual blues voice, a voice often at odds with the collective. As the blues, Sula is an embodiment of life's emotional territories, and is neither good nor evil. Sula's life and the novel's story, are a dialectic synthesis of antithetical forces--the physical and emotional pain and torment of life and the joy of life--brought together in a single subject. The "comforting conclusion" I am suggesting, therefore, is that as blues expression Sula is less like "any artist with no art form" (p. 121) and more like an art form whose existence is a painful reminder of life's moral indifference.

LeRoi Jones has also claimed that: "the term *blues* relates directly to the Negro, and his *personal* involvement in America.... *Blues* means a Negro experience...."[21] An application of Jones' and Ellison's definitions of the blues, together with Baker's suggestive "blues matrix" and Gates' explication of Signifyin(g), validates a reading of *Sula* as blues-based. Interestingly, Morrison begins *Sula* with a description of the Bottom which does in fact define it in terms of the blues. In the opening pages of the novel, Morrison presents the image of a woman "in a flowered dress doing a bit of cakewalk" (p. 4) who is being observed by a white man from the nearby valley and by a group of fellow "black people." Morrison's woman performing a cakewalk evokes the following response: "The black people watching her would laugh and rub their knees, and it would be easy for the valley man to hear the laughter and not notice the adult pain that rested somewhere under the eyelids, somewhere under their head rags and soft felt hats, somewhere in the palm of the hand, somewhere behind the frayed lapels, somewhere in the sinew's curve" (p. 4). Morrison clearly implies the white man's understanding of what he sees is partial and incomplete and his response is empathetic, while the response of those blacks who are members of the Bottom's folk community is completely sympathetic. In the woman's cakewalk, they feel the emotional ambiguity of the blues. They *know* the blues because they have lived them. What the white man comprehends is the woman's outward "manner," not the metaphoric "matter" she represents. In this brief scene, Morrison is claiming the blues as the natural expression of African American culture, and as something extraneous to white America. Morrison is also restating that the blues are a confluence of the comic and the tragic, and that that is what the Bottoms is/was.

Sula herself is a character whose outlook on life is a direct reflection of the blues matrix, which is to say she can laugh in the face of pain, and she has the ability to make others laugh as well. For instance, there is the scene in which Jude, Nel, and Sula are talking and Jude laments that "a Negro man had a hard row to hoe in this world" (p. 103). Sula's response is characteristic of her blues outlook: she says to Jude, "I don't know what the fuss is about. I mean, everything in the world loves you. White men love you. They spend so much time worrying about your penis they forget their own. The only thing they want to do is cut off a nigger's privates. And if that ain't love and respect I don't know what is" (p. 103). Sula's humorous word play goes on to include white women and black women and how they feel about the "Negro man." Jude's and Nel's response is to laugh.

Sula's blues perspective and Jude and Nel's laughter mutually ease Jude's shame and indignation about not being hired for a job because of his race. What is easy to miss about Sula's blues point-of-view is that there is a touch of the trickster in all of this: Sula exercises a slight of hand (word) that has the effect of displacing sorrow and pain with amusement and diversion. It is Sula's quick wit that makes her light-hearted response to Jude's pain improvisation. Her outlook is at once an expression of the blues, and, a complex manipulation of language. The simple fact is that there is little difference which separates blues expression from that of the trickster--both are improvisational artists. The receptiveness of Sula's friends to her verbal improvisation is a reflection of their own innate sense of its cultural appropriateness, naturalness, and of its healing properties.

Sula's improvisational nature may appear to be a singular incident here, but there are others. In fact, Sula can respond as spontaneously as she does to Jude because much of her life has been governed by improvisation--a skill and legacy she has inherited from her grandmother, Eva Peace. What clouds the reader's estimation of that skill is that in Sula's improvisation, and in Eva's, there is a recognition of the self-serving trickster hiding behind the mask. Both women, for instance, mutilate themselves as a way of besting injustice as they perceive it. Eva Peace, it is well known to the characters in the novel, sacrificed her own leg for financial security. That is one improvisational way to beat a racist system; and it is a way of countering the effects of abandonment by her husband BoyBoy, who is but one of a string of irresponsible black males who populate this novel. Such is the blues/trickster legacy Sula inherits from her grandmother, and which she transforms during moments of crisis. For Sula, one such moment of crisis occurs when, along with Nel, she is confronted by the four white sons of Irish immigrants: Sula wards off their assault by self-mutilation. "Holding the knife in her right hand, she pulled the slate toward her and pressed her left forefinger down hard on its edge.... She slashed off only the tip of her finger" (p. 54).

When Eva Peace mutilates herself, she feels compelled to do so because her husband, BoyBoy, ran out on her. But, after she sacrifices her leg, Eva also finds that she is thereafter free of the demands of sex and, therefore, male domination. She has many male friends, but her sexual life is over. There is, therefore, a dual dividend in her mutilation: one is insurance money, the other is independence. In a blues sense, Eva finds a way to transform her crippling mutilation into an asset and a manifestation of power. The same is true of Sula's motives. Her self-mutilation has a double purpose. It helps to avoid a fist fight with the Irish boys and, because the scene occurs at the beginning of the girls' sexual maturation, it avoids the sexual assault that the narrative language implies. To continue quoting the above passage: "The four boys stared open-mouthed at the wound and the scrap of flesh, *like a button mushroom,* curling in the *cherry blood* that ran into the corners of the slate" (p. 54, emphases mine). Like her grandmother, Sula's self-mutilation has sexual significance--she is the one who forcefully breaks her own metaphorical hymen, releasing the flow of cherry blood, not some boy(boy)s. In this act Sula assumes sexual autonomy and independence from men. It is an act of disfigurement certainly, which leaves the reader confused. But it is also an act of courage, and an act of power. *It is also an act of improvisation--a way of acting which is not common or ordinary, an act of creative, self-defining possibility.*

No matter how "good" or "evil" Sula is perceived to be, while she is alive the blues are alive and the people of the Bottom survive despite personal and communal tragedy. When Sula dies, what follows is the death of the Bottoms: the community faces its own apocalypse. The novel's final chapter, set twenty-four years after the main body of the novel, is a recitation of the gradual destruction of the Bottom and the erosion of life there after the disastrous cave-in at the tunnel and, only one year before, the death of Sula. This chapter's purpose is to dramatize the emotional distance and disorientation that Nel feels after the Bottom's apocalyptic collapse. Her life goes on, but without much meaning, until she realizes in a kind of epiphany just how much Sula meant to her. As communal history, the novel *Sula* is an "oral" record of the Bottom's health and vitality with Sula serving as a visible, incarnate expression of African American life as expressed in the blues. When Sula dies, the folk life and folk expression of the Bottom becomes dislocated, loses it vitality, and perishes. Nel's final cry, her final knell, is an epiphany symbolizing her recognition of what Sula meant to her. And because, in her conventionality, Nel represents the Bottom, her cry must be seen as the cry of the lost community, too late realizing the value of what has been lost. Nel's cry is "pure blues expression"[22] because Sula is pure blues expression.

Nel's realization and recognition of loss ("'O Lord, Sula,' she cried, 'girl,girl,girlgirlgirl'" (p. 174)), ends the novel on a note of recovery. A recovery of value, a recognition of the thing lost which can be reclaimed. Nel's cry, which Morrison describes as a "fine cry," is caused, I am suggesting, by her implicit realization of the fact that to know and accept Sula was to know the blues. Casting Sula out of her life had caused Nel to live for years haunted by a "gray ball." Only by reclaiming Sula in her fine cry, does Nel recover her equilibrium. As an essential part of African American tradition and culture, the recognition of Sula's worth as blues and the recovery of that value are necessary for the health of African American culture. Nel does not articulate that point as I have, but the message, the moral of the Bottom's tale is implied if the novel is understood as an exploration of the blues and its place in African American life.

The blues, as a form of folk expression, cannot exist in a vacuum. For the blues to be viable and meaningful, they must be nurtured by a folk environment which understands the blues form as vernacular discourse. Stated another way, if the blues are to be intelligible and meaningful to the people of the Bottom, they must co-exist within a culture that values and perpetuates its folk customs. This folk heritage provides the context in which the blues function. In *Sula*, this cultural background is especially necessary. Actually, folklore not only sets the stage in which the blues can be acted out in *Sula*, folk life and folklore are the stage. It is not going too far to claim that *Sula* is told in a style that mimics the folk parable, the folk tale.

The novel never makes clear exactly when the Bottom, the ironically named hilly neighborhood near Medallion, Ohio, was first settled. But the preface chapter of the novel, the only one which does not bear a title (all subsequent chapters are titled with dates), relates the origins of the Bottom in a narrative style that resembles the fairy tale. The customary "once upon a time" opening is missing, but the story is about a place no longer in existence in a time that has passed. Further, the prefatory chapter which introduces Part One of the novel contains a simple creation tale which relates in a straightforward style and distant voice, the origins of the Bottom, the black neighborhood which serves as the setting of the novel. The fairy tale structure is reinforced when the origins of the Bottom are further elaborated upon as a "nigger joke" in which, the tale goes, after the abolition of slavery, "A good white farmer promised freedom and a piece of bottom land to his slave if he would perform some very difficult chores" (p. 5). This passage faithfully mimics the tone and language of any number of folk tales, and particularly the fairy tale, in which a reward is promised to a person who can successfully complete a difficult task. The "nigger joke" comes in when the freed slave tries to claim "his piece of bottom land." The devious white master "tricks" the slave into believing that the fertile bottom land he had won wasn't as good as the "bottom" up on top of a hill. He tells the doubting slave: "'High up from us,' said the master, 'but when God looks down, it's the bottom. That's why we called it so. It's the bottom of heaven--best land there is'" (p. 5). The slave, the reader is asked to believe, gullibly falls for the story and lays claim to a lifestyle and a legacy that is difficult and backbreaking.[23]

The creation myth about the Bottom sets the stage and tone for the rest of the novel. On one hand, the tale evokes both the formulaic pattern of challenge/reward of folk tales and myth which it then undercuts with irony; but also, and just as importantly, the opening chapter retells another familiar story--that of the trickster being tricked. There is no evidence in Morrison's handling of the slave's duping to suggest the slave had himself been a trickster, but there is such a strong affinity in African American lore of the trickster with the slave, that such a comparison is not unreasonable. The Bottom is henceforth destined to become a community of blacks who find themselves tricked into believing the promises of white America; and as a result, their lives become a legacy of trouble and travail. Ultimately, their false hopes lead them to their deaths. (Another reading of this event could argue that the slave hadn't learned how to respond to the white man in a manner that is double-voiced, that somehow would have allowed the slave to receive his due without offending the white man. Possibly the slave hadn't learned how to signify in this manner, illustrating his literal and figurative uprootedness.)

This introductory chapter establishes foremost the language of the blues: the trickster tricked and the later denizens described as laughing to hide their pain (p. 4). These elements combine to create a blues atmosphere, an awareness that this is a neighborhood that understands the nature of the blues, in fact lives the blues. This chapter also establishes the ongoing vernacular of the fairy tale, one of the types of lore Morrison will evoke many times in the novel.[24] The immature, indistinguishable dwarfs, the deweys, suggest the dwarfs of the Snow White. Chicken Little, who never gets the chance to warn "the sky is falling," suggests a single, ridiculous voice which believes that imminent danger surrounds the Bottom. Shadrack, whose name comes from the Bible's Book of Daniel, suggests the need for faith in the face of adversity. The tale of Jack and the Beanstalk is mentioned (p. 9), as is the suggestion of the Pied Piper of Hamlin (p. 159), both of which are trickster tales. Finally, both Nel and Sula are linked to fairy tale images of maidens being swept away by knights in shining armor (pp. 51, 52). What this listing of fairy tale sources implies is not that Morrison is derivative. She is not. But because of their immediate recognition, and because they are combined in a blues matrix, Morrison has readily established a fertile *folk* soil in which to plant her tale. As such the entire novel *Sula* can be read as a folk tale. And as a blues tale. It is a history. It is autobiography. It is a lesson. It has deep psychological reverberations. It has a moral.

Morrison is also careful to portray the major characters in folkloristic terms. Thus, like the creation tale retold about the Bottom, the tale of Shadrack, the first major character introduced in the novel, is also a folk tale. After Shadrack's war experience erases his personality, or his sense of it, he returns stateside to an army hospital for over a year to recover. Disoriented, and perhaps a little crazy, an episode of violence with a male nurse just so happens to coincide with a need for more bed space. Like the "nigger joke" that created the Bottom, in another "nigger joke," Shadrack is released without having fully recovered. But Shadrack's release is a release into a new world. Disoriented, he doesn't know where to go, where he is going. Morrison describes him as a man "...with no past, no language, no tribe, no source, so address book, no comb, no pencil, no clock, no pocket handkerchief, no rug, no bed, no can opener, no faded postcard, no soap, no key, no tobacco pouch, no soiled underwear and nothing nothing nothing to do..." (p. 12). With no past and no identity to lay claim to, Shadrack emerges from the hospital a blank slate. This is his creation tale. When the police finally pick him up and throw him in jail, it is in a toilet bowl that Shadrack first sees who he is. "There in the toilet water he saw a grave black face. A black so definite, so unequivocal, it astonished him. He had been harboring a skittish apprehension that he was not real--that he didn't exist at all. But when the blackness greeted him with its indisputable presence, he wanted nothing more" (p. 13). Realizing who he is, or at least what he is, Shadrack falls into a deep sleep, which Morrison describes in a mixture of lyrical images that combine flight and the seeds of genesis: "the pits of plums...the condor's wing...the curve of eggs" (p. 14). When he is released from the jail, Shadrack hitches a ride on the back of a wagon, significantly loaded with squashes and pumpkins--vegetables full of seeds. This entire episode is thus a creation myth, like the one told in the preface chapter describing the origins of the Bottom. First Morrison creates a place, and then she creates a person to live there. The characteristics of folklore and folk life are thus established early on in the novel. Of course, Shadrack is not the first inhabitant of the Bottom. The Bottom is well settled when he arrives. Yet he seems, in some ways, representative.

In many ways, Shadrack is also undeniably unique. His way of handling the anguish he feels about death is to institute "National Suicide Day." Falling on the 3rd day of January, Shadrack parades around town with a cowbell and hangman's rope. Certainly Shadrack's National Suicide Day is an act of signifying. Shadrack's holiday mocks white America's New Year's Day celebration of success. It inverts the New Year's icons to suggest the blues perspective of suffering amidst the promise of plenty, of death (by lynching) at a time of new hope and promise. At first wondered at and shunned, eventually Shadrack's annual performance ritual becomes part of the calendar. As he parades he goads his detractors with curses which "were stingingly personal" (he is playing the dozens). Eventually, Shadrack's "annual solitary parade" becomes part of the folk consciousness, becomes part of the Bottom's folk lore: "...they had simply stopped remarking on the holiday because they had absorbed it into their thoughts, into their language, into their lives" (p. 15).

What Morrison has done in two very brief, very compact chapters, is to establish a neighborhood in which folklore and folk life are viable. There is a very real sense of history about the Bottom and its principle inhabitants. The Bottom's creation tale is retold in a language that is mythic and folkloristic; the same is true about Shadrack. Wherever he originally came from (and here the reader might justifiably assume Africa), he is deposited in a new world without an identity, but with a history. Shadrack's creative imagination provides a fertile soil for folk legend and folklore. No matter what else the reader may feel about Shadrack, he comes to the new world of the Bottom something like a blues priest, capable of performing the annual rites which "celebrate" the African American experience in America, laughing in the face of death, because not to laugh would mean giving up hope.

To display the range of cultural values competing within the Bottom, Morrison focuses on two family groups. Each represents a dichotomy of values. Together, the Wright and the Peace households represent, respectively, what James H. Evans, Jr., has called "the culturally uprooted and the culturally grounded." This term, which Evans used in his discussion of Morrison's *Song of Solomon*, applies equally well to *Sula* (and *The Bluest Eye*, as Chapter IV illustrated). Evans' description:

The central problem which the characters face are determined
by the extent to which they are culturally grounded or
culturally uprooted. Cultural grounding refers to the capacity
of a character to draw sustenance from the indigenous
environment. Cultural uprooting refers to the incapacity of a
character to draw upon those resources.[25]

As Morrison presents the novel, Eva Peace and her household represent
the "culturally grounded," and Helene Wright represents the "culturally
uprooted." Evans cautions against viewing these two elements as strict
opposites; rather Morrison *juxtaposes* these forces to furnish "the
literary force of the narrative."[26] What follows is a discussion of
Morrison's portrayal of Helene Wright (and her cultural uprootedness).
        Blackness does not guarantee a folk heritage or a sense of
black pride (a topic already explored by Morrison in *The Bluest Eye*).
In the chapter titled "1920," the reader is introduced to the Wright
family, particularly the child Nel and her mother Helene. Helene has a
number of pretensions, not the least of which is that she is superior to
the other blacks of the Bottom. Raised by her grandmother because her
mother was a prostitute in the red-light district of New Orleans, Helene
is out of touch with her past and disdains anything that reminds her of
her own low origins and her own daughter's negroid features. Indeed,
Helene is so far displaced from the Bottom's cultural center that she is
unable to make the inhabitants of the Bottom call her Helene; they call
her simply "Helen," signifying her inability to "name" herself. One
aspect about Helene's character is that she is determined to undermine
her daughter's enthusiasms, which Helene equates with wild blood.
"Under Helene's hand the girl became obedient and polite. Any
enthusiasms that little Nel showed were calmed by the mother until she
drove her daughter's imagination underground" (p. 18). In Helene's
mind, wild blood is the legacy Nel inherits from Helene's mother, the
prostitute, and which she is determined to drive "underground."
        The illness of her grandmother causes Helene to return to New
Orleans, taking a long train ride south, accompanied by her daughter
Nel. Leaving the sequestered safety of the Bottom, the trip is a return
to the Jim Crow life of segregation. It is a trip Helene is ill-prepared
for. Mistakenly boarding her train on the "Whites Only" coach, Helene,
who is a "pale yellow woman," does not disembark and walk to the
"Colored Only" car. Instead, she makes her way directly through the

white car to the colored one. Along the way, she is interrupted by the white conductor who asks her, "What you think you doin', gal?" (p. 20).[27]

Like the ex-slave whose labors earn him the Bottom, Helene finds herself caught in a situation her verbal skills are unable to untangle. Helene's difficulty stems from the fact that she has not learned the culturally taught verbal skills necessary to deal with these racial situations. Helene's mistake is compounded when she smiles at the conductor who has put her in her place. Were Helene better equipped to handle Jim Crow laws and those who impose them, she might have conducted herself in a manner that would have preserved her dignity and pride. But she does not. Instead, her smile is overseen by the black men in the next car, and their tacit criticism and disdain is her reward. There is no "puttin' on the massa'" here; and no assumption of a feigned "Aunt Jemima" mask which (as in the hands of the character Pilate in Morrison's later novel *Song of Solomon)* might have redeemed her. Helene is ill-equipped to deal with racism because of her pretensions and because she lacks the culturally acquired vernacular skills to support her. Her boarding of the white car is itself evidence of her loss of sense of place and propriety. Helene further exhibits how out-of-touch she is on the train by not comprehending, until suffering hours of discomfort, that the only bathroom available to her is the field beyond the railroad track.

Not surprisingly, when Helene arrives in New Orleans, she is too late. Her grandmother has already died. The significance of her late arrival is that, "The old woman had died without seeing or blessing her granddaughter [Nel]" (p. 25), displaying another lack of cultural continuity in the Wright household. There is no blessing and no heritage to pass along to Nel. Helene even refuses to speak Creole, the tongue of her family. What the trip illustrates to the reader is Helene's cultural uprootedness, her self-imposed displacement from her family and her heritage. In her pride, she has renounced her family, her folk culture, and the larger African American experience as well. In every situation she encounters on the trip, she behaves either badly or inappropriately.

Nel, who is ten years old at the time of the trip, learns that she has no desire to be looked at as disdainfully as her mother was by the black soldiers on the train. The travel has also widened her sense of the world. Like Shadrack looking in the toilet water and seeing himself for the first time, Nel returns home to the Bottom and looks in a mirror and sees something that she hadn't seen before: herself.[28] "'I'm me,' she whispered. 'Me'" (p. 28). In an archetypal sense, the journey is a trip of self-discovery. The trip, in spite of her mother's failures, gives Nel a glimpse of her roots and her heritage. The trip also gives Nel the courage to discover for herself a soul-mate whom her mother would surely disapprove of: Sula Peace.

After describing the Wright household and Helene's distance from the center of the Bottom's folk life, the chapter "1921" introduces the Peace family to the novel. The matriarch of the family, Eva, is introduced via a folk-like tale. Like the integration of Shadrack's "National Suicide Day" into the Bottom's mythos, the loss of Eva Peace's leg is also part of the Bottom's legends. And like the bifurcated nature of the blues, the loss of Eva's leg represents both tragedy and triumph. The tragedy is not only the physical loss of her leg, but also that her husband had abandoned her and their small children necessitating her sacrifice. The triumph is that the sacrifice of her limb for insurance money represents a successful playing out of the trickster, of a black woman somehow "puttin' on the massa'" to the tune of $10,000.

The tale and speculation about Eva's sacrifice becomes part of the Bottom's folklore; and it represents the extent to which African American women will go to be good mothers and providers for their children. But there is a great deal more to this tale. For as a result of her sacrifice, Eva achieves a number of things: financial security; an honored place in the community; and an ascendancy to a makeshift throne, made of a rocker and child's wagon, from which she is able to direct the lives of her family and her boarders. And she gains sexual independence from men.

Unlike Helene Wright, who is intent on forgetting her mother's prostitution and denying that there is anything "common" about her, Eva Peace naturally and unwittingly passes on her sexual attitude (legacy) to her daughter Hannah and granddaughter Sula: "...those Peace women loved all men. It was manlove that Eva bequeathed to her daughters" (p. 41).[29] Eva Peace also has the power to name. It is she who gives names to Tar Baby, the deweys, and she has nicknames for two of her three children: she calls Eva "Pearl," and Ralph "Plum." (Readers will recall the absence of nicknames in the Wright household; indeed, Helene is not able to get the people of the Bottom to call her anything but Helen.)

The essential purpose of chapter "1921" is to introduce the Peace family as a contrast to the Wright family. There is no doubt that

Helene Wright is not at peace with herself, her ancestry, her place as an African American. In contrast, the Peace household displays a family of (primarily) women who are able to cope with the world as it is, to enjoy it, and to make the best of what they have. They are adapters. Survivors. Improvisors. And by example, their matriarch, Eva, teaches her family how to survive. She is a combination of many things not so common: she is a trickster; she is sexually independent; she has the power to name; and she exercises the power of life and death. She is a strong women who gains much of the power she has from her acceptance of her role as a good provider and sacrificing mother.

Part of the reason Eva can lay claim to her esteemed position in the Bottom is that Morrison is careful to explain how Eva first came there. Originally, Eva came to Medallion and the Bottom along with her husband, BoyBoy. He had come as a carpenter's assistant, asked to accompany his boss from Virginia. Like the black farmer whose labor earned him the Bottom, BoyBoy also was conned into following a false dream; he too was tricked into believing that a white man would do right by him. In the novel's third "nigger joke," BoyBoy finds himself in the Bottom, out of work. As BoyBoy's wife, Eva's tale has ironic significance. It at once confirms that she has lived in the Bottom long enough to be one of its insiders. However, she was also once an outsider by birth--a point not without importance when considering Sula's role as pariah, and the theme of Eva's legacy to Sula.

Eva also has the power to give and take life--a rather dubious power she will pass on to Sula. This is a troubling power, fraught with moral ambiguity, especially as readers' perceive it, and as Morrison displays it in Eva's interactions with her son Plum. When Plum was a baby, constipation threatened to kill him. Eva took Plum to the outhouse and with the last bit of lard left in the can, inserted her finger into his bowel to release the pent up stools. In an act of love and motherly intimacy, Eva saved Plum's life. Years later, however, after Plum returned from the war, a heroine addict, Eva burned Plum to death, killing him before he can destroy himself totally, or do what Eva claimed: "he wanted to crawl back in my womb and well ... I ain't got the room no more even if he could do it" (p. 71). Eva commits a horrible crime, but for a good reason--or so she argues. It is not what she does here that matters, but why. The reader is asked to recognize the fact that Eva can, in committing so vicious a crime, actually do it for love's sake.

It is into this blues/folk environment, and out of these two dissimilar households that Sula Peace and Nel Wright come. Sula emerges from a family with a rich folk legacy it is not ashamed of; Nel emerges from a family that is small-minded and detached from the Bottom's common folk. From the chapter "1922" on, the novel explores the development of these two children, and in doing so probes the never-ending tension that exists between the culturally grounded and uprooted, the conventional and the iconoclastic, the collective and the individual.

Chapter "1922," presents two major subjects: one is the sexual maturation of Sula and Nel; the other is Sula's "killing" of Chicken Little. These are not isolated themes: they are interwoven in the presentation Morrison creates. For it is the women in *Sula* who are the purveyors of culture and part of their acculturation process is determining what has value and what does not.

The two young girls are now friends and share a number of fantasies, particularly, daydreams of a "fiery prince" who will rescue them from their loneliness. Part of their exploration of their budding sexuality is to walk to the ice cream shop and past the men who loiter at the shops nearby. The girls' sexuality is then displayed in the sexual language, already referred to, to describe Sula's self-mutilation.

In that signal act of self-mutilation, Sula demonstrates the lesson she has learned from Eva: suffering is the unavoidable price for independence. This lesson is reinforced in the following incident: It is in the summer of her twelfth year that Sula overhears her mother, Hannah, and some other women discussing the travails of raising children. At the point of the discussion that Sula overhears, her mother says, "...I love Sula. I just don't like her" (p. 57). Sula does not understand her mother's words, or, more importantly, their meaning. She reacts by running down to the river with Nel, and there, the two girls lie in the grass and dig a hole with a stick. The imagery is sexual, phallic. As the girls play with the grass:

> Sula lifted her head and joined in the grass play. In concert, without ever meeting each other's eyes, they stroked the blades up and down, up and down. Nel found a thick twig and, with her thumbnail, pulled away its bark until it was

stripped to a smooth, creamy innocence. Sula looked about and found one too. When both twigs were undressed Nel moved easily to the next stage and began tearing up rooted grass to a make a bare spot of earth....soon [Nel] poked her twig rhythmically and intensely into the earth, making a small neat hole....Sula copied her....When the depression was the size of a dishpan, Nel's twig broke. With a gesture of disgust she threw the pieces into the hole they had made. Sula threw hers in too....[then they added] paper, bits of glass, butts of cigarettes, until all of the small defiling things they could find were collected there. Carefully they replaced the soil and covered the entire grave with uprooted grass. (pp. 58-59)

This entire scene is an act of veiled sexual initiation. Nel, without knowing it, is playing out her life and the life of so many other women of the Bottom: in an act of play, she is foreseeing her life as wife, a life in which the initial pleasures of sexuality give way to a sense of defilement and misuse (abuse).

Sula's life is not a mirror of Nel's, despite their compatibility. Sula has come to this initiation scene in a state of active bewilderment because of overhearing her mother's comment about not liking her. Sula plays along with Nel, digging the hole and filling it with objects of defilement, but her personal state of mind is more complex. After covering this little "grave" with grass, Sula takes a small boy, Chicken Little, up to the top of a tree to show him the view. This excites Chicken Little, but the trip back down the tree terrifies him. When he is finally coaxed down, Sula spins him around so hard that she loses her grip and Chicken Little is hurled into the nearly river, where he drowns.

This scene is a particular puzzlement because, as a character in the novel, Sula only *acts* here; she does not explain her actions. How people *act* is, of course, one of the problems of the novel. How do we interpret the actions of the characters? *Sula* is not a novel of introspection or deep psychological insights. Readers do not have the benefit of probing dialogue. Because of *Sula*'s folktale simplicity, characters must be judged by their actions, not motives. The reader is, therefore, left to wonder: Is Sula's drowning of Chicken Little an accident? As a signifier of the blues, her experiences are meant to be a reflection of life's extremes, its ups and downs, its tragedy and triumph. Sula-as-blues assumes a social role which functions to ameliorate and transcend any philosophical stance which emphasizes life's negatives. In this regard, Chicken Little's name is no accident. His namesake, from popular lore, is the little chicken who, upon being struck by raindrops, calls out that the sky is falling. As a symbolic character with a symbolic name, Chicken Little represents those people who make a disaster out of the natural. In her role as blues, Sula thus eradicates this one-sided, chaotic, and unnatural, world view.

Given the character of this chapter, the death of Chicken Little can further be seen as a kind of ritualistic (initiation) sacrifice. For it is in this same chapter that Sula mutilates herself to avoid a beating at the hands of the Irish boys, a beating which clearly had sexual overtones. Thereafter, Sula overhears her mother say she loves, but does not like Sula. Next comes the "sexual foreplay" in the grass. All these scenes come in a chapter which is clearly meant to demarcate the sexual maturation of both girls. By mutilating herself, Sula clearly acts out her knowledge (gained from Eva) that from pain comes the pleasure of independence. Sula, who is aware of this paradox in a physical sense, learns that same lesson in an emotional sense, from her mother's comments: life, like raising children, is something one can love, but not like (the lament of the blues restated). And whereas the grass play foreshadows Nel's life as traditional, Sula has come to a realization that women need not be defiled by men. They have in fact a power over men. Sula has learned that lesson already, too, when Eva killed Plum rather than allowing him to defile her (or himself) any further. Sula allows Chicken Little to experience a feeling of ecstasy and then she snuffs that pleasure out. Not out of evil intent, and not to see what it feels like to kill someone. But as a condition of her own experience as a woman: she has the power to give life and to take it away. This too is a restatement of the blues: life is a constant interplay of hope and loss.

Chicken Little's death and Sula's role in it repeats a style of initiation rite similar to that of Shadrack. The novel does not reveal Shadrack's past before WWI, but we can assume that his terrifying experience with death changes him into the human being presented in the novel. His war experience serves as an initiation, an initiation so terrifying it leaves him nearly senseless for a year and, thereafter, causes him to begin his annual rite, Suicide Day. The link between Sula and Shadrack is more explicitly made when, fearing Shadrack has seen the drowning, Sula ventures to Shadrack's shack where, somehow, Shadrack acquires Sula's belt, which he keeps for years.

If Chicken Little's death poses problems of interpretation, Hannah's death does no less so. In the chapter "1923," Hannah's death is preceded by a number of omens, "strange things," which forecast something ominous: there is a strong wind without rain; Hannah dreams of a red bridal gown; there is Sula's strangeness, now that she is thirteen; and Eva can't find her comb. Perhaps even odder, is Hannah's questioning Eva about Eva's love for her children, and asking why Eva killed Plum. Hannah's question angers Eva; but more importantly, it gives Eva--in a rare instance in the novel--a chance to explain why she murdered her own flesh and blood. The end of Eva's response is this: "I done everything I could to make him leave me and go on and live and be a man but he wouldn't and I had to keep him out so I just thought of a way he could die like a man not all scrunched up inside my womb, but like a man" (p. 72). This is one of the very few times in the novel that Hannah is engaged in dialogue and there is, as a result, something artificial about her questioning Eva. It should be noted too that when Hannah is questioning Eva, she is shucking peas--that is, performing the literal manifestation of Eva's response: removing seeds from a pod (womb) from whence they can never return. Metaphorically, her labor is a manifestation of Eva's explanation for killing Plum--Eva killed Plum because he wanted to return to the womb, which is an unnatural act. The encounter between the pea-shucking Hannah and Eva allows Morrison to give a literal characterization to a metaphysical problem. And it allows Eva a chance to vindicate herself.

African American novels are full of incidents in which mothers killed their children during slavery times to free them from a life of bondage. Morrison, in fact, would explore this theme in her later novel, *Beloved* (1987). The portrayal of a slave committing suicide to avoid a continued life of slavery, also was common. In the African American tradition, the idea of murder or suicide as a solution to a life of hell, is not only a metaphysical question--is it a real option (a fact which Shadrack's National Suicide Day ritualized).

What is most curious about this encounter between mother and daughter is that not only is it one of the few times Hannah actually reveals her personality through speech, but she also reveals how little she understands personally about the blues. For in her question, "Mamma, did you ever love us?" (p. 67), she reveals her failure to understand and perceive her mother's past actions as signifying sacrifice. She, it seems, does not understand an essential irony of life: that to love and to like life are not the same thing, *despite the fact that she herself has confessed feeling the same emotions about Sula* (p. 57).

Not long after this scene, Hannah burns to death in a grass fire while canning vegetables in the back yard. Eva hurls herself out of her third-story window in a futile attempt to rescue Hannah. As Eva recollects the incident, she recalls seeing Sula on the back porch, "just looking," as her mother burns to death. Sula's failure to come to her mother's rescue is a prickly matter. As a character in the novel, Sula's failure to act earns her Eva's scorn and distrust. It is also the source of numerous critical assessments which claim Sula is evil. But as a symbol of the blues, Sula's distant observation of the tragedy is a reflection upon her role as blues signifier: she must witness (and give witness to) the tragedies of life, but not necessarily be able to overcome them.

In the next chapter, "1927," after Nel Wright marries Jude Green, Sula leaves the Bottoms. The marriage of Nel and Jude is by no means presented as a full partnership of two fully-developed characters. And yet, the marriage is what closes the first half of the novel. Ending the first part of the novel with the marriage of Nel appears on the surface to be a conventional narrative technique. It suggests a neat, clean ending to the first half of the tale. But that is not the case. For what the first half of the novel has accomplished is to establish the characters of Nel and Sula as both closely aligned, yet dramatically disparate. Nel, as a member of a conventional, socially conscious household, succumbs to her mother's expectations and marries. Sula, on the other hand, after growing up in the Peace household, is neither conventional, nor ready to settle down. She, as it turns out, is very much the opposite of Nel. Nel opts for convention, marriage, children, and definition as the wife of a man; Sula opts for independence, singleness, no children, and self-definition. And whereas one single train trip is enough to convince Nel that she has seen and experienced the world, Sula sets off for parts unknown to broaden her horizons. Thus the first half of the novel ends with a closure for Nel and an opening for Sula.

The first half also concludes by establishing the kind of intimacy Nel needs, and the distance from involvement which Sula requires to sustain herself. During the first half of *Sula*, Morrison has used the language of folk narrative to build a community and breath life into its society. In doing so, she has realized two types of possibility in the Bottom: Nel and her ilk rely on others for definition; Sula is able to define herself, and thus serves as a measure for the others who live in the Bottom to gauge themselves against. Sula-as-blues, by necessity, must be both good and bad, sacred and profane. She must be large enough as character and as symbol to serve as the Bottom's bell-weather. The Bottom needs Sula to assess the success and meaning of their own lives. Sula as blues, is, therefore, both attractive and repulsive, both tragic and transcendent. The first half of the novel established in folk language the environment of the Bottom, and its principle members; it also established two families whose values and sense of heritage are at odds.

The second half of *Sula* is a study of disintegration: Sula moves Eva to a rest home; Sula ruins Nel's marriage; Sula dies; the Bottom comes to ruin. When Sula makes love to Ajax, she envisions herself removing layers of his body, his bone giving way to gold, to alabaster, to soil. Her vision resembles the ancient dream of Nebuchadnezzar (Daniel 2: 32, 33) which Daniel interprets as the crumpling of the Babylonian empire. Before Sula dies, she has her own dream of disintegration:

> Then she had the dream again. The Clabber Girl Baking Powder lady was smiling and beckoning to her, one hand under her apron. When Sula came near she disintegrated into white dust, which Sula was hurriedly trying to stuff into the pockets of her blue-flannel housecoat. The disintegration was awful to see, but worse was the feel of the powder.... (p. 147)

In this wide course of erosion, even Sula's birthmark, most often referred to as a rose (a rose symbolically being "a symbol of completion, of consummate achievement and perfection"[30]), is described more often in this part of the novel, and it too is perceived as changing: to Nel is seems darker (p. 96) but still resembling a stemmed rose (pp. 138, 144); to Jude it is a "copperhead" (p. 103); to the members of the Bottom it assumes the shape of "Hannah's ashes" (p. 114) and an "evil birthmark" (p. 115); to Shadrack it seemed once to be a "tadpole" (p. 156).

Despite the novel's insistence that Sula is evil--"In their world.... The presence of evil [Sula] was something to be first recognized, then dealt with, survived, outwitted, triumphed over" (p. 118)--Sula is not responsible for the Bottom's collapse. This cautionary tale, told in the 1970s about a time when racism was pervasive in America, has the subtle intention of warning contemporary blacks about placing too much faith in the economic promises of White America (evidenced in the "nigger jokes" for instance)--especially at the cost of desecrating African American culture as epitomized in the blues.

The retention of a blues outlook on life is central to Morrison's story. As in Part One of the novel, Part Two also opens with a blues statement. In the fourth paragraph of Part Two, Morrison again restates the Bottom's philosophical outlook: "The purpose of evil was survive it and they determined (without ever knowing they had made up their minds to do it) to survive floods, white people, tuberculosis, famine and ignorance. They knew anger well but not despair..." (p. 90). Faith in this blues outlook is always subject to strain in the Bottom and Sula's return to the Bottom forces its members to re-evaluate the roles of family, marriage, and self. Sula's presence also forces Nel, more than anyone else, to progress from a state of "pre-individual" existence to a state of existential "essence." Sula forces Nel to define herself and in the process to discover what about her life is important.

The shattering of Nel's complacency begins with Sula's affair with Nel's husband, Jude, which ruins Nel's marriage and, Nel believes, her life. Nel is devastated because she expected her marriage to provide stability to her life. Or, to use a recurrent word in the novel, Nel wants things to be: "always." As Nel laments in her grief about losing Jude: "Sula was wrong. Hell ain't things lasting forever. Hell is change" (p. 108). Sula-as-blues, as improvisation, is an affront to such longings.

Nel has invested her life in the conventional roles of wife and mother, roles which even the novel's narrative voice depicts as limiting. Without Jude to define her purpose, Nel's grief manifests itself in ways which display Nel's weak personality and which sharply contrast with Eva's handling of like situations. For instance, in her grief over Jude, Nel finds herself in the bathroom all bound up with emotions she cannot express; her crisis in her bathroom recalls Eva's trip to the outhouse with baby Plum. Nel's bathroom scene is described this way:

> ... The bathroom. It was both small and bright, and she wanted to be in a very small, very bright place. Small enough to contain her grief.... Once inside, she sank to the tile floor next to the toilet. On her knees, her hand on the cold rim of the

bathtub, she waited for something to happen ... inside. There was stirring, a movement of mud and dead leaves.

Hunched down in the small bright room Nel waited. Waited for the oldest cry. A scream not for others, not in sympathy for a burnt child, or a dead father, but a deeply personal cry for one's own pain. A loud, strident: "Why me?" The mud shifted, the leaves stirred, the smell of overripe green things enveloped her and announced the beginnings of her very own howl.

But it did not come. (p. 108)

Nel also regresses to a state of near-infantile fear and begins to sleep with her children: "For a long time she could not stop getting in the bed with her children and told herself each time that they might dream a dream about dragons and would need her to comfort them. It was so nice to think about their scary dreams and not about a ball of fur" (p. 109). Nel's sleeping with her children provides contrast to Eva's rationale for killing Plum--she feared his re-entry into her bed.

In these parallels, Eva acted in ways which were, arguably, unselfish and justifiable; Nel's actions, however, are the result of insecurity and are a sign to the reader that Nel and the Bottom are losing their center, are becoming "dislocated." The members of the Bottom fear Sula because she makes them change. Sula's "experimental life" makes their lives experimental. In short, Sula-as-blues, Sula as improvisation, terrifies the Bottom. And yet, the Bottom has a life philosophy which is blues oriented. They just don't seem to realize the similarities. My conclusion is that the Bottom has lost its sense of the blues' proper place in their lives. The Bottom has lost its center. The evidence of this surfaces when Nel loses Jude. It is at that point that the narrative suddenly shifts from third-person to first-person. The end of chapter "1937" becomes Nel's lament, her first-person blues song in which she bemoans the loss of her man. Ironically, Nel doesn't recognize that she is singing the blues:

And what am I supposed to do with these old thighs now, just walk up and down these rooms? What good are they, Jesus? They will never give me the peace I need to get from sunup to sundown, what good are they, are you trying to tell me that I am going to have to go all the way through these days all the way, O my god, to that box with four handles with never nobody settling down between my legs.... I could be a mule or plow the furrows with my hands if need be ... if I knew that somewhere in this world in the pocket of some night I could open my legs to some cowboy lean hips but you are trying to tell me no and O my sweet Jesus what kind of cross is that? (p. 111)

In the next chapter, although Sula is described in nullifying terms by the novel, the description nonetheless seems apt for Sula-as-blues. Morrison writes about Sula that: "She had no center, no speck around which to grow.... [and]--no ego" (p. 119). Despite Morrison's description, it is in this chapter that Sula's role is given a new dimension. For it is only now that she doffs her role as symbol and becomes human enough to desire Ajax and experience the blues herself.

Ajax is described as a man who loves two things: his conjure-woman mother and flight. He is not frightened by a strong woman. And so he goes to meet Sula at her home, looking at her "through the *blue glass*" of her front door (p. 127, emphasis added). As a result of their affair, Sula changes, and while she once loved or desired nothing, now she does: "Sula began it discover what possession was. Not love, perhaps, but possession or at least the desire for it" (p. 131). After Ajax leaves her, Sula discovers she didn't know Ajax well enough to know his real name was Albert Jacks. Holding his driver's license in her hand, Sula goes to bed:

...she crawled into bed and fell into a sleep full of dreams of *cobalt blue*.

When she awoke, there was a melody in her head she could not identify or recall ever hearing before. "Perhaps I made it up," she thought. Then it came to her--the name of the song and all its lyrics just as she had heard it many times before. She sat on the edge of the bed thinking, "*There aren't any more new songs and I have sung all the ones there are. I have sung them all. I have sung all the songs there are.*" (p. 137, emphases added)

The novel's suggestion that Sula is ready to die because she has no new experiences to live for is a plotting device, and not especially convincing. Nonetheless, the fact that Sula lives in a house with blue glass and has dreams of cobalt blue signifies that Sula is linked to the blues. Immediately following this scene, in the next chapter, we learn that Sula is deathly ill. Her ensuing death becomes: "... best news folks up in the Bottom had had since the promise of work at the tunnel" (p. 150). Soon thereafter, the rumor of blacks being used to work on the tunnel becomes an "announcement" and the people of the Bottom take this to be a good omen relating to the death of Sula. But this happy augur soon turns sour as an ice storm blankets the city, showering ruin on everyone.

Then Medallion turned silver. It seemed sudden, but actually there had been days and days of no snow--just frost--when, late one afternoon, a rain fell and froze.... They ... gazed at the sun pressed against the gray sky like a worn doubloon, wondering all the while if the world were coming to an end....

Late-harvesting things were ruined, of course, and fowl died of both chill and rage....

The consequence of all that ice was a wretched Thanksgiving of tiny tough birds, heavy pork cakes, and pithy sweet potatoes. By the time the ice began to melt and the first barge was seen shuddering through the ice skim on the river, everybody under fifteen had croup, or scarlet fever,...

Still it was not those illnesses or even the ice that marked the beginning of the trouble.... there was something wrong. A falling away, a dislocation was taking place. Hard on the heels of the general relief that Sula's death brought a restless irritability took hold. (pp. 152-53)

Hard on the heels of Sula's death, Chicken Little's implied warning has come true: The sky is falling! Without Sula, without Sula-as-blues to provide the Bottom's equilibrium, the disintegration, the "dislocation," takes hold. Even the Bottom's families begin to lose their coalescence: "Now that Sula was dead and done with, they returned to a steeping resentment of the burdens of old people. Wives uncoddled their husbands; there seemed no further need to reinforce their vanity" (pp. 153-54).

And in what becomes the greatest improvisational act of the Bottom's history, Shadrack's final Suicide Day ends in disaster, as numbers of citizens release their pent up frustration and drown in one mass regrettable action. This apocalyptic event is not the result of a failure of the blues, but the failure of misplaced hope: the misplaced hope that from outside of the community economic salvation would come. The drownings are an expression of a lack of faith in the philosophy of the blues--that things will get better, not as a result of fulfilled hopes, but because they can't get any worse.

> ...they called to the people standing in the doors... to help them open this slit in the veil, this respite from anxiety, from dignity, from gravity, from the weight of that very adult pain that had ungirded them all those years before. Called to them to come out and play in the sunshine--as though the sunshine would last, as though there really was hope. The same hope that kept them picking beans for other farmers;... kept them convinced that some magic "government" was going to lift them up, out and away from that dirt, those beans, those wars. (p. 160)

Sula-as-blues did not offer hope, but humor. Sula-as-blues also provided a mirror in which a people could see themselves, define themselves, and laugh in the face of misery. It is the failure to recognize this about Sula that causes the dislocation of the Bottom. And it is this that Nel realizes twenty-four years later, in 1965. Then, after "the Bottom had collapsed" (p. 165) and Nel "had pinned herself into a tiny life" (p. 165), Nel is finally released from the gray ball that has dogged her when she realizes that it wasn't Jude that she missed all those years, but Sula. "It was a fine cry" Nel makes, coming finally to realize who and what she is, and what is important. The cry she could not make years earlier in her bathroom (p. 108), becomes the book's final note, a note of recovery, a fine blues note sung about a lost love: Sula. *Sula* as novel becomes in the final analysis a blues song: "an autobiographic chronicle of personal catastrophe expressed lyrically."

NOTES

1. *Sula* (New York: Plume, 1982). All references to this text are to this edition and are denoted by number in parentheses.

2. *The Signifying Monkey: A Theory of African-American Criticism* (New York: Oxford University Press, 1988). All textual citations to this text are from this edition and are denoted by number in parentheses.

3. Robert B. Stepto, "'Intimate Things in Place': A Conversation with Toni Morrison," *Massachusetts Review* 18 (1977): p. 475.

4. Ibid., p. 475.

5. Ibid., p. 478.

6. "Like an Eagle in the Air: Toni Morrison," *Modern Critical Views*, ed. Harold Bloom (New York: Chelsea House Publishers, 1990), p. 127.

7. "Self, Society, and Myth in Toni Morrison's Fiction," *Contemporary Literature* 23, no. 3 (summer 1982): p. 14. Rpt. in *Modern Critical Views: Toni Morrison*, Ibid., pp. 7-25.

8. "A Hateful Passion, a Lost Love," *Modern Critical Views*, Ibid., p. 28.

9. Ibid., p. 29.

10. *Blues, Ideology, and Afro-American Literature: A Vernacular Theory* (Chicago: University of Chicago Press, 1984), p. 146.

11. "A Hateful Passion, a Lost Love," Ibid., p. 28.

12. The term "pre-individual" as I use it takes its meaning from Ralph Ellison's essay on Richard Wright's novel *Black Boy*. Ellison traces the term "pre-individual," to "the young Negro critic, Edward Bland." See *Shadow and Act* (New York: Vintage Books, 1972), pp. 77-94, 83.

13. *Long Black Song: Essays in Black American Literature and Culture* (Charlottesville: University Press of Virginia, 1972), p. 16.

14. *Blues, Ideology, and Afro-American Literature*, Ibid., pp. 3-4.

15. Ibid., pp. 134, 135, 135.

16. Morrison has called Sula "improvisational" in her essay "Unspeakable things Unspoken: The Afro-American Presence in American Literature," *Modern Critical Views: Toni Morrison*, Ibid., p. 223.

17. "The Seer and The Seen," *Shadow and Act*, Ibid., pp. 78-79.

18. Jean-Paul Sartre, "Existentialism is a Humanism," *The Existentialist Tradition: Selected Writings*, ed. Nino Langiulli (Garden City, NY: Anchor Books, 1971), p. 393.

19. "A Hateful Passion, a Lost Love," Ibid., p.29.

20. *Blues People: The Negro Experience in White America and the Music That Developed From It* (New York: Morrow Quill Paperbacks, 1963), pp. 66-67.

21. Ibid., p. 94.

22. Keith E. Byerman, "Beyond Realism: The Fictions of Toni Morrison," *Modern Critical Views: Toni Morrison*, Ibid., p. 70.

23. Whether this ex-slave was gullible or not is a matter of futile debate here because not enough is known about him to make that judgment. What may also be the case is that the ex-slave realized he was in a no-win situation, both rhetorically and actually, in which his own language skills were of no use. The failure of language, especially in situations which present "paradoxes of communication," can occur across cultural lines. Jay Mechling is especially helpful in describing how African American language skills have helped blacks deal with whites and with members of their own culture by teaching blacks how to deal with "the double bind" of language's literal and figurative meanings. A brief example: Mechling explains that when Richard Wright's black boy literally kills a cat because his father said to, his father finds that to punish his son for taking his words literally, instead of their intended figurative meaning, would undermine his own authority. As a result, Black Boy gets the better of his father and escapes punishment, too ("The Failure of Folklore in Richard Wright's *Black Boy*," in *Journal of American Folklore* 104, no. 431 [summer 1991]: pp. 275-94).

24. Trudier Harris discusses "the formulaic opening of fairy tales" as one of the oral sources used in the structuring of *Sula*, in her

Fiction and Folklore: The Novels of Toni Morrison (Knoxville: University of Tennessee Press, 1991), pp. 53-55.

25. *Spiritual Empowerment in Afro-American Literature* (Lewiston, NY: Edwin Mellin Press, 1987), p. 133.

26. Ibid., p. 133.

27. Helene's cultural displacement is further dramatized by her ignorance of trains and their operation, a common subject of blues songs. As Langston Hughes relates "These lovers of the open road [blues singers], in their desire for the far country, turn to the train as their best friend." See *The Book of Negro Folklore* (New York: Dodd, Mead & Co., 1983), p. 379.

28. As mentioned earlier, Houston Baker recognizes this as a signal moment in the development of the individual's black consciousness--that moment when black people recognize that they represent a "zero image" in white America, and thus need to rewrite who they are in their own terms. See *Blues, Ideology*, Ibid., pp. 145-57.

29. Robert Palmer, in his work *Deep Blues*, relates part of a blues song sung by "a spunky little pianist named Louise Johnson ... [who sang] some very naughty blues, one of which celebrated in fairly graphic detail the joys of having sex standing up. 'I'm goin' to show all you women,' she bragged, 'honey, how to cock it on the wall.'" Hannah's penchant for having sex standing up is passed on to Sula, who opts to use that position the first time she and Ajax make love: "...holding the wet milk bottle tight in her arm she stood wide-legged against the wall and pulled from his track-lean hips all the pleasure her thighs could hold." Whether this taste for sex standing up is the result of a blues influence, or a matter of sexual politics, I will not venture to judge (New York: Penguin Books, 1982), pp. 78-79, 125.

30. J.E. Cirlot, *A Dictionary of Symbols*, Second Edition, trans. by Jack Sage (New York: Vail-Ballau Press, Inc., 1983), p. 275.

CONCLUSION

In my first chapter, I placed more emphasis on the socio-historical content of the slave narratives than on their artistry and merit as literature. I did so for two reasons. One was to contest the failure of scholars to treat African American literature as a unique voice in our literature. Secondly, it is impossible, *not* to read the slave narrative as social documents. This does not mean that they should be regarded as verbatim factual accounts; it does mean that they provide extraordinary testimony to the social and personal conditions of slavery. To emphasize their historical nature does not mean that I would go as far as Robert Bone did, and claim that "the quality of these works does not justify intensive literary analysis."[1] I strongly disagree with his general critical dismissal of African American literature predating 1890. American literary scholars study Benjamin Franklin's autobiography seriously, why should we not give slave narratives the same critical attention? Indeed, the 1990 publication of a collection of essays about Frederick Douglass[2] attests not only to the historical significance of slave narratives, but also to the attention contemporary literary scholars now give them.

Bone also suggested that African American literature improves artistically the farther its progresses from its early stages (the slave narratives). Perhaps that is what African American scholars and writers have implied when they claimed that it was not until the 1960s that blacks were writing for blacks, and were, therefore, free of the racial baggage of having to worry about a white audience and its reaction to or rejection of its work. By that time, artistic considerations were able to supersede others. To argue whether or not the early works are as artistic as the contemporary novels under consideration here is moot. Tastes change, as do aesthetic considerations. But, if writing for an audience whose culture is not completely your own is like fighting with

133

an arm tied behind the back, then these early works can be seen as even more remarkable achievements.

In my introduction, I suggested some of the characteristics which differentiate the nineteenth and twentieth century works discussed here. To this list, I would add their relative treatment of religion. The slave narratives were written for evangelical Christians and relied on anti-Christian ironies for part of their effectiveness. Therefore, Christianity claims a major and positive thematic role in those works. Walker's works, on the other hand, move away from Christianity toward humanism, a move that is evident in *The Color Purple*. Even more surprising, Toni Morrison's novels barely make religion an issue. Serious attention to Christianity is almost nonexistent in her works. In her portrayal of the African American community it is the folk beliefs of the group which provide world view, ontology, and eschatology, not Christian doctrine.

If character development is an integral part of the slave narrative tradition, both in terms of educational advancement and economic well-being (as is the case with the narratives of Frederick Douglass and Booker T. Washington), then Alice Walker's works bear a more striking similarity to these literary ancestors than Morrison. *Meridian* and *The Color Purple*, like the narratives, are highly chronological, emphasize positive character development, the overcoming of oppression, and are ultimately hopeful--meaning that her heroines serve as models for others. Like Douglass and Washington, Walker's female protagonists overcome enormous obstacles. Morrison's novels, in contrast (with the notable exceptions of Milkman Dead in *Song of Solomon* and Nel's epiphany in *Sula*), de-emphasize character development. Nor do her characters, as directly as Walker's, confront the twin evils of sexual and racial oppression.

In the modern novels examined here, Walker's stance is the more political. Issues of racism, political activism, and the effects of colonial capitalism in the Third World are her major themes. And yet, her works are also intensely personal. In Meridian Hill's and Celie's biographies we find stories of growth against formidable odds. In *Meridian*, the men are sexist and self-centered, so it is against the social conventions that suppress women and limit their role to that of mothers and wives, that Meridian Hill must rebel. In *The Color Purple*, with the help of a strong, independent woman, Celie discovers the courage to rebel against the conventional roles she has been assigned by men. In

Walker's novels, the individual heroine faces a number of demons: racism, patriarchy, sexism, and a folklore that supports them. Yet her women triumph. Her women may be weak and vulnerable at the onset of their ordeals, but they acquire mythic stature by the end of their stories. In other words, Walker's novels are moral. She writes with political and moral intent. Her women overcome the problems and obstacles they face, and when they do, they serve as models for other women, and for men.

We may wish to call this kind of writing, in which moral and social dilemmas are resolved, "idealistic," in the sense that it combines realistic portraits of daily living with a measure of political wish fulfillment. And to some extent that is true. Walker's novels move toward a kind of idealism in which her heroines triumph and reshape their world. What is especially idealistic about *The Color Purple* is the breadth of change which Walker effects. But it is not just women who concern Walker; she is also determined to refashion the men and make them more sensitive partners. Thus we see that in *The Color Purple*, Mr.___ must undergo a spiritual regeneration, just as Meridian Hill must in *Meridian*. In each novel, these characters regress, become nearly infantile, and then are resurrected in spirit through the power of forgiveness. Walker's literature is a literature of hope. She takes her culture's folklore and its conventions and recasts them, indeed, reinvents them so that the next generation will be better than the current one.

What idealism is there in the novels of Toni Morrison? Very little. Perhaps that is a measure of her artistic vision. Of the two women, her novels are certainly the more lyrical. But Morrison's characters are not as well developed as Walker's. Walker's Celie and Meridian grow immensely in their novels; and so too do the novels' men, Mr.___, Harpo, and Truman Held. If characterization is a measure of artistic success, Walker surpasses Morrison easily.

Morrison, perhaps, earns more praise than any other African American woman writer, however, for her ability to saturate her fiction with what Trudier Harris has called "a folkloristic aura." Harris also praises Morrison's creative talent for "the unusual twists she gives to her use of folklore [which places her] at the forefront of contemporary black authors who are consciously creating new myths and new ways of perceiving what we mean by 'folk.'"[3] Harris is correct. Whereas Walker utilizes African American folklore to give cultural depth to her characters (which is to say, she integrates the folklore directly into her writing), Morrison uses the structure of folklore, its signifying language, and its formulaic patterns to fashion works which create new folk lores. She is in this regard, as Harris calls her, "folkloristic." Harris also appears to classifying Morrison as a Romantic, in the sense that Hawthorne had defined it (as that literary place "where the Actual and the Imaginary meet"), although she never labels her that. But the label seems apt, especially if we extend the scope of Morrison's writings under consideration beyond the two herein, and include *Song of Solomon* and *Beloved*, with their ghosts and spirits playing active roles (called by the oxymoron, "Magic Realism").

For all her artistry, however, Morrison has relied on two narrative techniques which she repeats in her novels. One technique is her use of signifying characters. Another technique is the polarization of characters into groups which are either culturally grounded or uprooted. In the Breedloves and the Mac Teers, the Wrights and the Peaces, we discover the oppositional forces of African American culture at odds. On the political field, the two groups resemble the long-standing antagonisms of the assimilationists and the black nationalists, although they are not presented in those terms.

Unlike Walker, whose novels work toward a resolution, Morrison's novels are open-ended. In her novels, forces confront one another and provide the dramatic energy which drives them forward. But they do not drive toward a conclusion. Reading Morrison's novels is emotionally stressful due to the constant tensions her characters confront and embody. Unlike Walker, whose characters gradually better themselves (thereby relieving the empathy readers feel for them), the representational nature of Morrison's portrayals demand a strong, unmitigated empathy. Reading Morrison is, at times, like watching a long, drawn-out battle which no one can win: she offers no neat solutions to the drama of our lives.

Finally, while both these writers use the blues, their usage varies significantly. Walker is less critical of the blues' emphasis on the individual voice as it conflicts with the values of the group. She romanticizes the blues figure (ie., she emphasizes their positive side), the way Langston Hughes does with his blues-singing character Harriett in *Not Without Laughter*; their common approach is to view the blues singer's folk origins as proof of his or her value to the community as an expression of its continuity and strength. Morrison's usage is more complex. For while she utilizes the blues to illustrate the rootedness of her characters, she conversely emphasizes, as in Cholly and Sula, the blues' ironic association with the "black blues life," the solitary voice which threatens the continuity the group. As a strong individual voice, these blues characters appear to threaten the safety of the community.

The works examined in this work present a bleak portrait of the African American family. In *Meridian*, a young mother abandons her husband and child to pursue an education. In *The Color Purple*, a "father" rapes his daughter and gives her two children away. In *The Bluest Eye*, a father rapes his daughter, and the daughter goes mad. In *Sula*, an entire community perishes because it loses its connection with its heritage. But to summarize these novels in this way is as fallacious as trying to paraphrase a poem: it is impossible to due justice to the complexity of these works by reducing their artistic complexity to a single plot summary.

And that is just as well. There are so many currents and counter-currents in these works that it is impossible to finally come to any single conclusion about them. Other than to say they are exceptional art. Which brings me finally back to where I began: asking what is unique about African American literature? Henry Louis Gates, Houston Baker, and Toni Morrison, among others, rightly claim that what makes African American literature unique is its manipulation of language and meaning, its signifying complexity, and its unique narrative style, combining standard English with black English vernacular. Throughout this study, I have tried to answer that question in another way, by comparing and contrasting the themes of African American literature to other American literature. I hope it is clear that while African American literature does have unique concerns, its primary concerns and artistry transcend all attempts to confine it to the literary margins. It is, as Ralph Ellison said, universal.

NOTES

1. Introduction to *The Negro Novel in America* (New Haven, CT: Yale University Press, 1958), p. 8.

2. Eric Sundquist, ed., *Frederick Douglass: New Literary and Historical Essays* (Cambridge: Cambridge University Press, 1990).

3. *Fiction and Folklore: The Novels of Toni Morrison* (Knoxville: University of Tennessee, 1991), p. 190.

BIBLIOGRAPHY

Andrews, William L. *The Literary Career of Charles W. Chesnutt.* Baton Rouge: Louisiana State University. Press, 1980.

------. Foreword to *The House Behind the Cedars,* by Charles Chesnutt. Athens, GA: University. of Georgia Press, 1988: vii-xxii.

Awkward, Michael. "Roadblocks and Relatives: Critical Revision in Toni Morrison's *The Bluest Eye.*" *Critical Essays on Toni Morrison.* Edited by Nellie Y. McKay. Boston: G.K. Hall & Co., 1988: 57-68.

Baker, Houston A., Jr. *Blues, Ideology, and Afro-American Literature: A Vernacular Theory.* Chicago: University of Chicago Press, 1984.

------. *The Journey Back.* Chicago: University of Chicago Press, 1980.

------. *Long Black Song: Essays in Black American Literature and Culture.* Charlottesville, VA: University Press of Virginia, 1972.

Baldwin, James. *The Fire Next Time.* New York: Dell, 1964.

------. *Go Tell It On The Mountain.* New York: Signet, 1954.

Baldwin, Richard E. "The Art of *The Conjure Woman.*" *American Literature* 43, no. 3 (November 1971): 385-98.

Bell, Yvonne R., et.al. "Afrocentric Cultural Consciousness and African-American Male-Female Relationships." *Journal of Black Studies* 21, no. 2 (December 1990): pp. 162-89.

Bettelheim, Bruno. *The Uses of Enchantment: The Meaning and Importance of Fairy Tales.* New York: Knopf, 1976.

Bluestein, Gene. *The Voice of the Folk.* Amherst: University of Massachusetts Press, 1972.

Bone, Robert. *The Negro Novel in America.* New Haven, CT: Yale University Press, 1958.

Brent, Linda [Harriet Jacobs]. *Incidents in the Life of a Slave Girl.* Edited by L. Maria Child. New York: Harcourt Brace Jovanovich, Publishers, 1973.

Brown, William Wells. *Clotel; or, The President's Daughter [with a Sketch of the Author's Life]*. New York: Citadel Press, 1969.

Byerman, Keith E. "Beyond Realism: The Fictions of Toni Morrison." *Modern Critical Views: Toni Morrison*. Edited by Harold Bloom. New York: Chelsea House Publishers, 1990: 55-84.

Campbell, Joseph. *The Hero with a Thousand Faces*. Second Edition. Princeton: Princeton University Press, 1973.

Cather, Willa. *My Antonia*. Boston: Houghton Mifflin, 1977.

Chesnutt, Charles Waddell. *The Conjure Woman*. Ann Arbor: University of Michigan Press, 1969.

------. *The House Behind the Cedars*. Athens, GA: University of Georgia Press, 1988.

------. *"The Wife of His Youth" and Other Stories of the Color Line*. Ann Arbor: University of Michigan Press, 1969.

Cirlot, J. E. *A Dictionary of Symbols*. Second Edition. Translated by Jack Sage. New York: Vail-Ballou Press, Inc., 1983.

Clarke, John Henrik. "Black Americans: Immigrants Against Their Will." *The Immigrant Experience in America*. Edited by Frank J. Coppa and Thomas J. Curran. Boston: Twayne Publishers, 1976: 172-191.

Coppa, Frank J., and Thomas J. Curran, eds. *The Immigrant Experience in America*. Boston: Twayne Publishers, 1976.

Davis, Cynthia A. "Self, Society, and Myth in Toni Morrison's Fiction." *Contemporary Literature* 23, no.3 (summer 1982): 323-42. Rpt. in *Modern Critical Views: Toni Morrison*. Edited by Harold Bloom. New York: Chelsea House Publishers, 1990: 7-25.

Davis, Thadious M. "Alice Walker's Celebration of Self in Southern Generations." *Women Writers of the Contemporary South*. Edited by Peggy Whitman Prenshaw. Jackson: University of Mississippi Press, 1984: 39-53.

Dixon, Melvin. "Like an Eagle in the Air: Toni Morrison." *Modern Critical Views*. Edited by Harold Bloom. New York: Chelsea House Publishers, 1990: 115-42.

Douglass, Frederick. *Narrative of the Life of Frederick Douglass*. New York: Signet, 1968.

Dorson, Dorson M., ed. *Folklore and Folklife: An Introduction*. Chicago: University of Chicago Press, 1972.

DuBois, William E.B. *The Souls of Black Folk. The Negro Classics*. New York: Avon Books, 1965.

Ellison, Ralph. "The Art of Fiction: *An Interview*." *The Black Novelist*. Edited by Robert Hemenway. Columbus, OH: Charles E. Merrill Publishing Co., 1970: 205-217. Rpt. in *Shadow and Act*: 167-83.

------. *Invisible Man*. New York: Vintage Books, 1972.

------. *Shadow and Act*. New York: Vintage Books, 1972.

Erickson, Peter. "Identity in the Work of Alice Walker." *College Language Association Journal* 23 (summer 1979): 71-94.

Evans, James H., Jr. *Spiritual Empowerment in Afro-American Literature*. Lewiston, NY: Edwin Mellin Press, 1987.

Farnsworth, Robert M. Introduction to *The Conjure Woman*, by Charles Chesnutt. Ann Arbor, MI: University of Michigan Press, 1969.

Farrison, William Edward. Introduction to *Clotel*, by William Wells Brown. New York: Citadel Press, 1969.

Faulkner, William. *Light in August*. New York: Vintage Books, 1972.

Garland, Hamlin. *Main-Travelled Roads*. New York: Signet Classic, 1962.

Gates, Henry Louis, Jr. "From Wheatley to Douglass: The Politics of Displacement." *Frededrick Douglass: New Literary and Historical Essays*. Edited by Eric J. Sundquist. Cambridge: Cambridge University Press, 1990: 47-65.

------. *The Signifying Monkey: A Theory of African-American Literary Theory*. New York: Oxford University Press, 1988.

Gibson, Donald B. *The Politics of Literary Expression: A Study of Major Black Writers*. Westport, CT: Greenwood Press, 1981.

Gidden, Nancy Ann. "'The Gray Wolf's Ha'nt': Charles W. Chesnutt's Instructive Failure." *College Language Association Journal* 27 (June 1984): 406-10.

Giles, James R. "Chesnutt's Primus and Annie: A Contemporary View of *The Conjure Woman*." *Markham Review* 3 (February 1972): 46-49.

Glaspell, Susan. "A Jury of Her Peers." Rpt. in *Literature: Structure, Sound, and Sense*. Third Edition. Edited by Laurence Perrine. New York: Harcourt Brace Jovanovich, Publishers, 1978: 377-93.

Harris, Joel Chandler. *Uncle Remus: His Songs and Sayings*. Edited with an Introduction by Robert Hemenway. New York: Penguin, 1982.

Harris, Trudier. *Exorcising Blackness: Historical and Literary Lynching and Burning Rituals.* Bloomington: Indiana University Press, 1984.

------. *Fiction and Folklore: The Novels of Toni Morrison.* Knoxville, TN: University of Tennessee Press, 1991.

Heermance, J. Noel. *William Wells Brown and Clotelle: A Portrait of the Artist in the First Negro Novel.* Hamben, CT: Archon Books, 1969.

Hemenway, Robert. Introduction to *Uncle Remus: His Songs and His Sayings,* by Joel Chandler Harris. New York: Penguin Books, 1982: 7-31.

Herder, Johann Gottfried von. "National Genius and the Environment." *Reflections on the Philosophy of the History of Mankind* 1784-1791. Edited and abridged by Frank E. Manuel. Chicago: University of Chicago Press, 1968: 3-78.

Hovet, Theodore R. "Chesnutt's 'The Goophered Grapevine' as Social Criticism." *Black American Literature Forum* 7 (fall 1973): 86-88.

Hughes, Langston and Arna Bontemps, eds. *The Book of Negro Folklore.* New York: Dodd, Mead & Co, 1983.

------. Introduction to *Pudd'nhead Wilson,* by Mark Twain. New York: Bantom Books, 1987: vii-xiii.

------. "The Negro Mother." *Selected Poems of Langston Hughes.* New York: Vintage Books, 1974.

------. *Not Without Laughter.* New York: Macmillan Publishing Co., 1969.

Hurston, Zora Neale. *Dust Tracks on a Road: An Autobiography.* Second Edition. Urbana: University of Illinois Press, 1984.

------. *Mules and Men.* Bloomington: Indiana University Press, 1978.

------. *Spunk: Selected Short Stories.* Berkeley, CA: Turtle Island Foundation, 1985.

------. *Their Eyes Were Watching God.* Greenwich, CT: Fawcett Publications, 1965.

Jacobs, Harriet. *Incidents in the Life of a Slave Girl: Written by Herself.* Edited by Jean Fagan Yellin. Cambridge: Harvard University Press, 1987.

Johnson, James Weldon. *The Autobiography of an Ex-Colored Man. Three Negro Classics.* New York: Avon Books, 1965.

------. "The Dilemma of the Negro Author." *The American Mercury* Dec. 1928: 477-81.

Jones, LeRoi. *Blues People: The Negro Experience in White America and the Music That Developed From It.* New York: Morrow Quill Paperbacks, 1963.

Kerber, Linda K. and Jane DeHart-Mathews, eds. *Women's America: Refocusing The Past.* New York: Oxford University Press, 1987.

Larson, Nella. *Passing.* Salem, NH: Ayer, 1986.

Lee, Harper. *To Kill a Mockingbird.* New York: Warner Books, 1982.

Levine, Lawrence W. *Black Culture and Black Consciousness: Afro-American Folk Thought From Slavery To Freedom.* New York: Oxford University Press, 1977.

Lewis, Richard O. "Literary Conventions in the Novels of William Wells Brown." *College Language Association Journal* 29 (December 1985): 129-156.

McDowell, Deborah E. "The Self in Bloom: Alice Walker's *Meridian.*" *College Language Association Journal* 24 (March 1981): 262-75.

McGowan, Martha J. "Atonement and Release in Alice Walker's *Meridian.*" *Critique* 23, no. 1 (1981): 25-36.

Mechling, Jay. "The Failure of Folklore in Richard Wright's *Black Boy.*" *Journal of American Folklore* 104, no. 431 (summer 1991): 275-94.

Meisenhelder, Susan. "'The Whole Picture' in Gloria Naylor's *Mama Day.*" *African American Review* 27, no. 3 (fall 1993): 405-19.

Morrison, Toni. *Beloved.* New York: Plume, 1988.

------. *The Bluest Eye.* New York: Washington Square Press, 1972.

------. *Song of Solomon.* New York: Knopf, 1977.

------. *Sula.* New York: Plume, 1982.

------. "Unspeakable Things Unspoken: The Afro-American Presence in American Literature." *Modern Critical Views: Toni Morrison.* Edited by Harold Bloom. New York: Chelsea House Publishing, 1990: 201-230.

Moses, Wilson J. "Writing Freely?: Frederick Douglass and the Constraints of Racialized Writing." *Frederick Douglass: New Literary and Historical Essays.* Edited by Eric J. Sundquist. Cambridge: Cambridge University Press, 1990: 66-83.

Mueller, William R. *Celebration of Life: Studies in Modern Fiction.* New York: Sheed & Ward, 1972.

Murray, Albert. *The Omni-Americans: New Perspectives on Black Experience and American Culture.* New York: Outerbridge & Dienstfrey, 1970.

Myers, Karen Magee. "Mythic Patterns in Charles Waddell Chesnutt's *The Conjure Woman* and Ovid's *Metamorphoses.*" *Black American Literature Forum* 13 (spring 1979): 13-17.

Nadelhaft, Ruth. "Domestic Violence in Literature: A Preliminary Study." *Mosaic* 17, no. 2 (spring 1984): 242-59.

Naylor, Gloria. *Mama Day.* New York: Vintage Books, 1989.

------. *The Women of Brewster Street.* New York: Penguin, 1983.

O'Brien, John. *Interviews with Black Writers.* New York: Liveright, 1973.

Palmer, Robert. *Deep Blues.* New York: Penguin Books, 1982.

Petry, Ann. "Mother Africa." *"Miss Muriel" and Other Stories.* Boston: Beacon Press, 1989: 126-62.

------. *The Street.* Boston: Beacon Press, 1985.

Pryse, Marjorie. "Zora Neale Hurston, Alice Walker, and the 'Ancient Power' of Black Women." *Conjuring: Black Women, Fiction, and Literary Tradition.* Edited by Marjorie Pryse and Hortense J. Spillers. Bloomington: Indiana University Press, 1985: 1-24.

Redding, J. Saunders. "The Negro Writer--Shadow and Substance." *The Black Novelist.* Edited by Robert Hemenway. Columbus, OH: Charles E. Merrill Publishing Company, 1970: 191-92.

Rowe, Karen. "Feminism and the Fairy Tale." *Making Connections Across the Curriculum: Reading for Analysis.* Edited by Patricia Chittenden, et.al. New York: St. Martin's Press, 1986: 629-35. Rpt. of *Women's Studies* 6 (1979): 237-57.

Sartre, Jean-Paul. "Existentialism is a Humanism." *The Existentialist Tradition: Selected Writings.* Edited by Nino Langiulli. Garden City, NY: Anchor Books, 1971: 391-416.

Sollors, Werner. *Beyond Ethnicity: Consent and Descent in American Culture.* New York: Oxford University Press, 1986.

Spillers, Hortense J. "A Hateful Passion, a Lost Love." *Modern Critical Views: Toni Morrison.* Edited by Harold Bloom. New York: Chelsea House Publishers, 1990: 27-54.

Stapleton, Michael. *A Dictionary of Greek and Roman Mythology.* New York: Bell Publishing Company, 1978.

Stepto, Robert B. "'Intimate Things In Place': A Conversation with Toni Morrison." *Massachusetts Review* 18 (1977): 473-89.

Stowe, Harriet Beecher. *Uncle Tom's Cabin.* New York: Signet, 1966.

Sundquist, Eric, ed. *Frederick Douglass: New Literary and Historical Essays.* Cambridge: Cambridge University Press, 1990.

Teller, Walter. Introduction to *Incidents in the Life of a Slave Girl,* by Linda Brent [Harriet Jacobs]. New York: Harcourt Brace Jovanovich, Publishers, 1973.

Terry, Eugene. "The Shadow of Slavery in Charles Chesnutt's *The Conjure Woman.*" *Ethnic Groups* 4 (1982): 103-25.

Toomer, Jean. *Cane.* New York: Liveright, 1975.

Twain, Mark. *The Adventures of Huckleberry Finn.* New York: Norton Critical Edition, 1962.

------. *Pudd'nhead Wilson.* New York: Bantom Books, 1987.

Walker, Alice. *The Color Purple.* New York: Harcourt Brace Jovanovich, Publishers, 1982.

------. *In Search of Our Mothers' Gardens.* New York: Harcourt Brace Jovanovich, Publishers, 1984.

------. *Meridian.* New York: Pocket Books, 1986.

------. *Possessing the Secret of Joy.* New York: Harcourt Brace Jovanovich, Publishers, 1992.

------. "The Revenge of Hannah Kemhuff." *In Love & Trouble.* New York: Harcourt Brace Jovanovich, Publishers, 1973.

White, Deborah Gray. "The Nature of Female Slavery." *Women's America: Reforming the Past.* Edited by Linda K. Kerber and Jane DeHart-Mathews. New York: Oxford University Press, 1987: 100-16. Excepted from "The Nature of Female Slavery," Chap. 2 of *Ar'n't I a Woman? Female Slaves in the Plantation System.* New York: W.W. Norton, 1985.

Wright, Richard. *Black Boy.* New York: Harper & Row, 1966.

------. *Native Son.* New York: Harper and Row, 1987.

Yellin, Jean Fagan, ed. Preface to *Incidents in the Life of a Slave Girl: Written by Herself,* by Harriet Jacobs. Cambridge, MA: Harvard University Press, 1987: vii-viii.

INDEX